How Firms Succeed 5.0

New Horizons for the Professional Services Firm

ISBN: 978-0-9885923-2-2

Östberg Library of Design Management
Greenway Communications, LLC, a division of The Greenway Group
25 Technology Parkway South, Suite 101
Norcross, GA 30092
800.726.8603
www.greenway.us

Layout and Cover Design: Austin Cramer

A DesignIntelligence Book

How Firms Succeed 5.0

James P. Cramer
& Scott Simpson

INTRODUCTION

When *How Firms Succeed* was first published in 2002, the A/E/C industry was poised at the brink of profound transformation, though it was not obvious to many people at the time. CAD, having been introduced in the early 1990s, was still a relatively recent phenomenon, but it was gaining widespread acceptance as the industry standard. Sustainable design, still in its infancy, was largely regarded a fringe movement and had not yet penetrated the mainstream of public policy. Most projects were constructed using hard bid or guaranteed maximum price contracts and were chronically delivered late and over budget, wasting billions of dollars each year. In those days, the bulk of the architect's fee was devoted to producing a commodity product — construction documents — and the cost of owning and operating a building after completion was scarcely considered during the design process.

It was in this context that *How Firms Succeed* first postulated the design/enterprise model of marketing/operations/professional services/finance, providing a framework for successful professional practice regardless of building type, project scale, location, or size of firm.

Today, things are much different. There has been a significant shift in how the profession and the public view sustainability. Issues of climate change, energy conservation, and carbon emissions have raised green design to a very high profile. It's become a central issue in public policy and has become big business, attracting billions of dollars of investment each year in venture funding. Scarcely a week goes by without major media coverage. In fact, sustainability has spawned a whole new generation of entrepreneurs who are eagerly seeking ways to harvest wind, solar, geothermal, and shale oil energy. In the process, U.S. dependence on foreign oil has dropped significantly.

Leapfrogging the CAD revolution, Building Information Modeling technology is fast becoming the new industry standard. Its ability to coordinate technical information across disciplines and to display images in 3-D format has revolutionized the ability of architects to explore and explain creative new design options. Even more important, BIM has changed the way the game is played. By making the design process transparent and easily accessible to every stakeholder (especially owners), it has radically altered the sociology of design. BIM puts a huge premium on collaboration and teamwork — two skills that in past years were relatively scarce among design professionals. It's becoming increasingly common for owners, architects, engineers, consultants, construction managers, and subcontractors to collaborate and share information using a single BIM platform.

The third big shift that has occurred over the past decade is something we call process innovation. It's not what we do as much as it is how we do it. Traditionally, the A/E/C industry has been organized into professional silos, and a measure of contention is built into the system. This is because, while there is a contractual relationship between the owner and designer and between the owner and contractor, there is no contractual relationship binding the designer and the contractor. It's a three-legged arrangement with one link missing. The obvious consequence is that pressure exerted on the owner tends to drive the architect and constructor apart. New forms of contracts and new protocols for collaborative project management, most commonly called Integrated Project Delivery, are beginning to transform the inherent contention into cooperation. Finally, the interests of all three parties are being brought into alignment with regard to the project goals, shared risks, and rewards. The result is that projects are being delivered with a much higher degree of predictability in terms of design quality, cost, and schedule. It's a breakthrough.

The overriding message is that by taking advantage of new technology and process innovation, the A/E/C industry is poised to deliver extraordinary value in ways that were never before possible. Design is both a verb and a noun; it deals with both process and outcome. Its effects are multi-dimensional and include not only aesthetics (form, massing, color, texture, light, etc.) but also time, capital cost, staff productivity, long-term maintenance and operational cost, and even branding. One need look no further than Apple — with its corporate culture driven by devotion to great design — to realize just how powerful this can be. In a mere 30 years, Apple has changed the way we live our lives and in the process has grown to be one of the most valuable corporations in U.S. history.

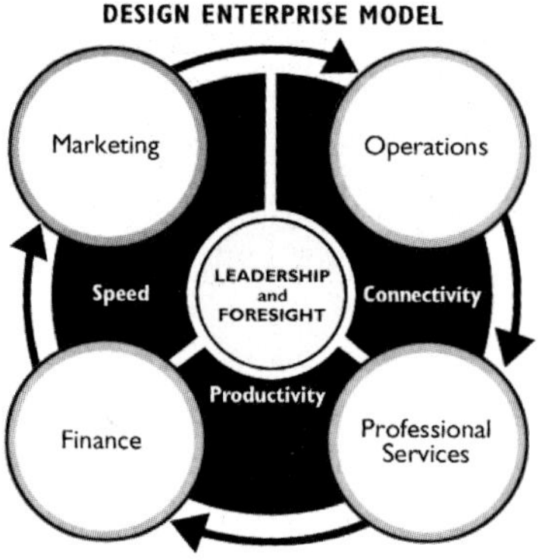

What does all this mean for the design professions? Everything. In the course of rewriting this book, we've taken a close look at the changes on the horizon and offer a refreshed perspective on how the A/E/C industry can and should respond. This is in essence the fifth generation/edition of *How Firms Succeed.* We've also found that the essential steps of the design/enterprise model (marketing, operations, professional services, and finance) still hold true. At the end of the day, it's about getting the work, organizing the workers, doing the job, and collecting the money. As in any endeavor, keeping the fundamentals in focus is the key to long-term success.

MARKETING:
GETTING THE WORK

The first step in doing great design is securing the commission. Marketing is the process by which the connection between design firm and client is created. No matter how talented or motivated the firm, without a client, it has nothing to do. Viewed this way, marketing is the first essential step in the design process. Through marketing, firms become intimately familiar with their clients and come to appreciate their goals, aspirations, resources, constraints, and decision-making processes. This includes understanding the parameters of scope, schedule, and budget that govern each and every project, no matter how large or small. Successful marketing is based on a few sound principles — listening well, communicating clearly, establishing credibility, articulating a value proposition and following through. Contrary to popular opinion, being good at marketing does not require a certain type of personality. Anyone who is properly motivated can do it well — all that is needed is to put the needs of the client first and foremost. The rest will follow.

Target Marketing: Pursuing the Right Projects for the Right Reasons

The purpose of marketing is to identify, attract, and retain clients for the firm. This can take a variety of forms, including advertising, public relations, speaking at conferences, publishing articles, responding to proposals, and contact with clients through a wide variety of organizations, both professional and non-professional. Smart marketing is a strategic investment, and the goal should be to produce maximum results for the investment required. Every aspect of marketing should be geared to communicating the value proposition of your firm: What does it do well, and how can this help the client?

How much does marketing cost, and what is it actually worth? These two questions are essential to assessing the overall effectiveness of your marketing program. To get the answers, start with the fundamental principle that if it costs more to bring in a job than you can earn by doing it, then your marketing — no matter how successful — will eventually drive you out of business.

No one can capture 100 percent of the market. In any given year, there is far more business to be done than any single firm can do alone. Therefore, one of the first and most important steps is to choose your targets carefully. Pursue only those projects for which your firm is uniquely qualified or is particularly well positioned. In simple terms, the best marketing strategy is to focus your energy on the work that you truly want. This is harder than it sounds because it requires a great deal of discipline to say no to an intriguing opportunity.

A few "starchitects" may have a waiting list of clients with significant projects but most are not so fortunate. There is a story, perhaps apocryphal, about Philip Johnson. A famous client sent Johnson a request for proposal and in return received the shortest winning proposal in history: "I'll do it." And he did. But most often, responding to proposals is not simple, and it is never cheap. Wasting time chasing jobs that you aren't likely to get and aren't really suited for diverts time and attention from the core mission of the firm. Such diversion is extraordinarily expensive, so avoid it at all costs.

To get a handle on how to choose, do a little research to determine your true cost of sales. The cost of sales is the expenditure in both time and materials needed to capture a dollar's worth of new net fee. The analysis can be done for specific markets or for individual projects. Most firms devote approximately five to seven percent of their annual net revenue to marketing, which means that their cost of sales ranges from five to seven cents on the dollar. The true figure can actually be much higher when opportunity cost is factored in. Activity devoted to unsuccessful pursuits is doubly expensive because that effort could have been used to support ongoing profitable projects.

When the true cost of sales has been determined, compare it to your average profit margin. This will tell you instantly which of the various market segments, projects, and clients make the most sense for your firm. It should be obvious that spending 7 percent of net revenue to compete for projects that average a profit margin of only 5 percent is not a winning strategy. At the very least, average profit margins should exceed the marketing cost. If not, then readjust the target mix of clients and projects.

The best and most productive marketing will occur when you are able to make a fit between the talent of the firm and the true needs of the marketplace. This requires discipline. Be honest about what you do well and celebrate it; successful marketing will follow naturally.

QUESTIONS

1. What is your true cost of sales?

2. What is your firm's hit rate in attracting new clients?

3. Based on actual results, who are your most effective marketers?

4. Before chasing a project, how will you know that you should?

"This solves everything! Now let's come up with a three-letter acronym so it fits in a sexy box."

Marketing: Setting the Tempo

Marketing works best if it becomes a normal, everyday part of your office culture. Reinforce the message that marketing is the first and most important step in design by starting each week with a marketing meeting. The message to all staff (especially those not directly involved in marketing) should be that marketing is a team effort and that everyone in the firm has a role to play. Explain that the firm will never stop looking, learning, and growing in ways that will strengthen the its ability to attract new clients.

It helps to focus the discussion with a simple summary or dashboard, updated each week, that lists the short- and long-term leads that are being chased, a record of the wins and the losses, and a graph that shows progress (both in terms of hit rate and the expenditure) benchmarked against the annual targets. This way, you'll know at a glance if you're "above-the-line" (ahead on wins and below budget), or "below-the-line" (watch out...you'll feel the effects three months later!). Each participant should make a brief report about current leads and contacts, recent marketing intelligence, and the strategy for specific clients and projects; a few minutes each is all it takes to bring everyone up to speed.

You'll be surprised at how much such a meeting can increase overall marketing effectiveness. It reinforces the team aspect of marketing and gives everyone a chance to contribute. Make sure that the marketing meetings are held in a visible place — the staff should know what's going on and why — and encourage anyone in the firm who has a contribution to make to attend, even on a periodic basis. Be sure to include younger staff, exposing them to your culture of client development.

The important thing is to demystify marketing. Make it everyone's business to help get work for the firm. Show by example that you value marketing and that you'll provide additional training and support for those who are especially interested or talented in this area. It's one of the best investments you can make.

QUESTIONS

1. How can you instill marketing as a firm-wide value?
2. Who should attend your weekly marketing meetings?
3. How do you quantify marketing success?
4. How will you get younger staff involved in marketing?

THE LANGUAGE OF MARKETING

Architects and clients are prisoners of their own unique languages. Architects are trained to think spatially and are comfortable interpreting plans, sections, and elevations, which embody the language of design. Clients generally think in terms of management, finance, and outcomes. It is rare to find a client who is adept at reading construction documents and equally rare to find an architect who is truly fluent in the language of business and finance, and yet both aspects are absolutely essential to the process of design and construction. The language barrier is real: it prevents both sides from understanding each other.

It does no good to blame the other party. If we want to be understood, we must learn to speak French while in France and German when in Germany. The trick is to find ways of expressing design value in business terms and business value in design terms. Here are some things that design professionals can do to lower the communication barrier:

1. **Learn to talk business talk.** Scan the local, national, and international business press, including the *Financial Times*, the *Wall St. Journal*, *The Economist, Fast Company*, and *Fortune*, and select one or two relevant articles each week. Write down three key points from each and add those to your daily conversations with clients and colleagues. Make this a lasting habit; it will pay big dividends.

2. **Never simply comply with a client request.** Always respond to requests with ideas or options that demonstrate how de-

sign thinking can benefit the client's bottom line. This is a great opportunity to infuse a new level of respect for how design can create business value for the client. Always deliver what you promise, and then provide an unexpected enhancement. Your long-term and repeat business will soar.

3. **Be direct and informative.** Your process skills as a designer are often misused or misunderstood. Clients frequently complain that architects and designers entertain false assumptions or take inefficient or unrealistic approaches to problem solving. Those who stand out have done their homework and understand the client's business issues, resources, and constraints. They know the right questions to ask. Clients need to know that the architect cares about the bottom line, and this reinforces the value of design. Learn to communicate in both business terms and design terms, and you will stand out from the crowd.

QUESTIONS

1. How will you communicate design value in business terms?
2. How will you re-brand your firm as business-friendly?
3. How will you better understand your client's needs in order to stand out from other firms?
4. How can you use business terms more often in your design practice?

MARKETING

One of the most basic concepts about marketing is that it needs to be cost effective. You can't live without it, but if you spend too much money bringing a job into the office, then even if the project is successful, you'll eventually drive yourself out of business. In evaluating your marketing costs, focus on your cost of sales. Simply put, this tells you how much you have to spend to bring in every dollar of new fees. Though this varies by firm size, location, and market focus, most offices spend around five to seven cents on the dollar to produce new work. Most important, remember that if your cost of sales exceeds your profit margin for that work, then you are on the road to failure.

Here's a simple way to create a pro-forma marketing budget for an architecture firm: Multiply the total number of staff in the office by $150,000 (the standard revenue benchmark per employee for architecture firms) and set the marketing budget at 5 to 7 percent of that figure. Remember that this must cover both labor and expenses. Then set your targets accordingly. For example, a 50-person firm will have to produce $7.5 million in new fees and spend no more than $525,000 in order to have a cost-effective marketing program. Keep within these basic parameters and you'll do fine.

While tracking your progress with regard to new booked work and ongoing expenses, don't forget that it's OK to exceed the marketing budget as long as you have the results to show for it. For example, you may choose to spend an additional $50,000 to pursue a dream project — this is no problem as long as you win. However, you must resist the temptation to spend marketing money based mainly on hope. Hope is not a strategy. To make the marketing budget work, you must exercise true discipline. This means that not going after a low-probability job is one of the best marketing decisions you can make. Instead, save those precious dollars for targets that you have a good chance of hitting. In other words, use a rifle, not a shotgun.

Here are some useful benchmarks when considering your marketing strategy:

1. The hit rate (ratio of new projects won as a percentage of those chased) should be at least 30 percent, meaning that you should get about one out of every three projects. Higher is better, of course. Various sectors and geographies result in different adjusted ratios.

2. New booked work per employee measured in net fees should be at least $150,000 annually. Some firms of all sizes are significantly higher.

3. Target your cost of sales at 5 to 7 percent of net revenue ($5,000 to $7,000 spent for every $100,000 in new fees produced).

4. Repeat business should be in the range of 65 to 75 percent each year. Higher is better because the cost of developing new business far exceeds the cost of developing repeat business.

5. Track which staff charges time to marketing and what new work is produced as a result. On average, principals should produce a minimum of $1.5 to $2 million in new net fees each year.

If you set a few clearly understood benchmarks and stick to your strategy, marketing will become second nature and part of your office culture.

Questions

1. How does your firm compare to the benchmarks on page 16?

2. How will you set your targets and track your progress for the coming year?

3. How will you improve your overall marketing results while lowering costs?

Marketing: Setting the Pace

Everybody in the firm — principals, support staff, technicians, interns — has an important role to play in the marketing process. Mindful that marketing is essentially about making the connection between what you do well and what the marketplace needs done, this means that every interaction or encounter can contribute to building those essential connections.

This starts at the front desk with the person who answers the phone and greets visitors. Is he or she courteous and helpful to all callers? Are clients' voices recognized? If the staff is temporarily unavailable — on the phone, at a meeting, or out of the office — does the receptionist know how to make them aware of the call as soon as possible? Are the staff who make outgoing calls using good phone etiquette? Do they treat everyone they talk to with courtesy and respect? Do they know how to use voice mail effectively? Are messages taken accurately and returned promptly?

Written communications are also critical, especially email. Are all letters and emails reviewed and corrected for spelling and grammar? Are meeting minutes issued within 24 hours? Are memos concise, accurate, and to the point?

Remember that every phone call, memo, letter, or voice mail is a brick in the wall of your reputation. Teaching your staff about good business manners and practicing them conspicuously yourself are very powerful aspects of your marketing reputation. Everything that touches a client leaves an impression.

Another essential business strategy is setting a good example in your personal interactions, both inside and outside the firm. If you get in the habit of treating everyone, especially your own staff, with courtesy and respect, you will reap the rewards in return. Extend this courtesy to everyone in your professional sphere — clients, consultants, and contractors as well as colleagues. Become known as a pleasure to work with, and in return you will attract clients who are also a pleasure to work with.

At every turn, demonstrate curiosity and helpfulness. When you read an article or a book that's of particular interest, circulate it to clients and staff who may benefit. When you return from a conference or a seminar, disseminate what you've learned. If you're always on the lookout for new ideas, you'll find more of them. And don't forget the small personal touches: A card or a call on a birthday shows special concern and makes a better connection than mailing out a thousand holiday cards, most of which are discarded after only a cursory glance. Build your own authentic rapport with those around you.

In all ways large and small, your behavior should show that you care about your clients and their concerns. Be on the lookout for ideas that may be useful to them. You want them to be successful because if they are, then you'll share in that success. Make this behavior part of your office culture, and you'll become a marketing powerhouse.

Questions

1. What is your marketing style?
2. What do your marketing brochures, website, and proposals really say about your value proposition?
3. How do you teach your staff about marketing skills?
4. How will you develop your own authentic marketing rapport?

Marketing: Attracting the Right Clients

To catch fish, you need the right kind of bait. You also have to be in the right spot and use the right equipment. So it is with marketing. Learn to go where the clients are, and have something useful to offer them. Ideally, you want to be in contact with clients before they need your services so that when the idea of a project first occurs to them, you'll already be on their radar screen and they'll naturally turn to you for help.

Strategic marketing is all about swimming upstream. Get in the habit of seeing yourself as a strategic advisor to your clients. Help them lay the groundwork for the project and establish the parameters of site, program, schedule, and budget. Do research on similar projects so that they'll know what to expect in terms of scope, schedule, and budget. Become aware of how they finance their projects. Offer to assist in writing their proposals if you can. Since the design and construction process is something of a mystery to most clients, become their guide so they'll know what to expect and what to avoid. If they see you as a partner in the process, you're well on your way to getting the job.

When marketing, stay alert for marketing "truffles." Truffles are those tasty little tidbits that are hard to ferret out but make the meal much more appetizing. When discussing a prospective project with a client, find out where the hard and soft spots are in the program, schedule, and budget and then start thinking of ideas and solutions that will address those issues. Learn how decision-making actually works in the client's organization so that when the project is underway, approvals can be obtained with a minimum of fuss. Get your clients to talk about their dreams — what's really driving this project? What do they stand to gain (or lose)? And while you're at it, plant a few truffles of your own. Help your clients realize that working with you will give them an edge.

Bear in mind that many people want to be an architect in some way, and they'll appreciate the chance to work with someone who will treat them as a true partner in the design and construction process. Remember that two imaginations working together are better than one and that dreams and aspirations are powerful motivators. In short, make a friend of your clients, and become their "co-conspirator." When clients see you as an extension of themselves, your odds of getting the job will approach 100 percent.

QUESTIONS

1. How will you swim upstream?

2. How will you become a "co-conspirator" with your clients?

3. How will you add strategic value to your clients' projects?

Marketing: Setting the Table

Once you've identified a project that you'd really like to get and have done the research and made personal contact with the client, then you must secure the commission. There are two basic approaches. The first is *process marketing*, in which the ultimate decision is made on the basis of pre-defined criteria and often includes requests for proposal and interviews. In such cases, you are usually competing against a long list of other firms, and all things being equal, your odds of winning are rather small no matter how qualified your firm may be. The second method is *network marketing*, in which the final decision is made on the basis of personal connections. (This also includes repeat business, which can easily account for 75 percent of your marketing success each year.) Network marketing is much more powerful and effective than process marketing for a very simple reason — all decisions in the selection process, on any job, are ultimately made by people. Clients do not hire strangers; they hire people, not business cards or brochures. They'll hire people they think will do the best job and people they trust the most. Hence, even process marketing has elements of network marketing embedded within it.

There are several rules of thumb that should govern all your marketing efforts. First, never respond to an RFP that comes in the mail unless you have prior knowledge of the project or a personal connection already established with the client. Generally, it's a waste of time. Instead, use that RFP to begin establishing a new relationship if you think that client has long-term potential. Second, never enter a design competition without a serious and objective evaluation of your chances for success. Competitions require an enormous expenditure of time and money, and the odds are not much better than pure chance. Because creating good architecture depends so much on a true process of engagement with the client, entering a design competition is somewhat like proposing marriage after the first date. It's a very risky way to establish a long-term relationship.

Third, pay very close attention to how the project will be financed. While it is true that form follows function, it is equally true that form follows finance. When you understand where the dollars are really coming from, you'll have an important key to the client's decision-making process. You'll also need to know how to use those dollars to the fullest advantage. If you don't know how a client expects to finance a project, just ask. This will be the first signal to them that you care about their precious resources. Follow up by doing some research using reliable data, and demonstrate that you understand how much similar projects should cost,. The message to clients is that good design embraces not only aesthetics and technology but also finance. By understanding all three, you can produce a better design. It's a very powerful marketing message.

Fourth, take the mystery out of marketing. It's really just a people-to-people process, and clients are real people, just like you. Talk to them in terms that they can understand, avoiding jargon. (Never say "fenestration" when "window" will do.) Be accessible, friendly, and curious. Offer your ideas freely without reservation. Promote the message in your firm that marketing — making that essential connection between what you want to do and what the market needs done — is everybody's business. When you do this, your marketing will become a lot more effective (and much more fun).

QUESTIONS

1. How will you become better at process marketing?
2. How will you become better at network marketing?
3. How will you discover clients' real decision-making process?

Planning for Marketing Success

Most firms over-invest but under-perform in marketing, and this has a tendency to produce three unfortunate outcomes: revenues remain stagnant, salaries lag, and profits are curtailed. Every firm should include marketing training as part of its strategic plan. Each employee should understand firm-wide marketing priorities and responsibilities. Here's how to promote this culture in your firm:

1. **Spend quality time with your clients.** Personal contact and follow-up notes and letters show that you care deeply about helping improve your client's condition. Aim for at least one interaction per month with each key client. Each one needs to be coordinated to fit your strategy. The firm message should be: "We care. We pay attention. We are part of your solution."

2. **Use weekly marketing meetings to drive the process.** Each member of the firm who is actively involved in marketing should report weekly on real prospects. For example, "Last week I had meetings with two current clients and two potential clients, sent articles to these prospects, and passed out our new firm brochure to three contacts at professional meeting." Understand the human connections and put more energy and enthusiasm into them.

3. **Spend more time researching potential projects and looking for the right fit.** Don't chase every new project that comes along; your time is too precious for that. Instead, invest time and energy where there appears to be a

good match. This will improve your hit rate substantially. Understand your potential client's business drivers and then you can add your own value.

4. **Implement a simplified time management system.** The system should remind you of each week's marketing priorities and action items. Track activities among all staff, focusing on how each person's effort can be synergistic with the overall strategy.

5. **Change your behavior.** Spend more time on marketing and be accountable for results, not just activity. Be hard-headed and soft-hearted. Don't just manage — lead your staff by example.

Establishing new marketing habits in the firm is easier for some than for others, but know that it is essential to your mission. Investing in smart marketing is far more effective than throwing money at a problem and hoping for the best.

> ***"The objective is constant market regeneration — one must embrace every change in the market as an opportunity ... change and get on with it."***
> DESIGN INTELLIGENCE

QUESTIONS

1. What role will you play in marketing?

2. How will you spend more personal time with clients and potential clients?

3. How will you change existing marketing behavior in the firm?

NURTURING YOUR RAINMAKERS

Rainmakers are people who nurture ongoing client relationships and are able to acquire key new projects for the firm. Every firm needs them. Accomplished rainmakers are hard to find. Those who can bring in work can be more valuable than those who actually do the work. Rainmaking and design ability are not necessarily mutually exclusive. Some leaders can acquire new business as well as deliver good design; in fact, in successful small firms this is often a necessity. It's important to understand that rainmaking can be taught. Every firm has younger staff with business development potential who have not been challenged to develop the necessary skills. They need training, nurturing, and encouragement. You can grow your own rainmakers by getting them involved in weekly marketing meetings, proposals, presentations, and key interactions with clients such as lunches or dinners. Encourage your staff to think beyond the four walls of the office.

What should you look for in a rainmaker?

1. A presence — someone who is noticed and respected (at any level in the organization).
2. A friendly and outgoing manner with an ability to communicate well.
3. A combination of assertiveness and persuasiveness.
4. A sincere interest in other people, both inside and outside the firm.
5. An intelligence that is admired but not overbearing.
6. The ability to think strategically about how the firm can add value for a client.

7. Healthy self-esteem — someone who does not take rejection personally.

Rainmakers can be hard to find and easy to lose. It's important that they are personally committed long term to the goals and strategy of the firm and that they communicate this belief at all times. Rainmakers are not sales people — they are driven by building long-term relationships.

Keeping rainmakers is a huge responsibility because the health of the firm depends on it. Special compensation frameworks are sometimes advisable. This can include a competitive base salary plus incentives based on both the volume of new business and the total profitability of the firm. Some rainmakers receive equity as a part of the total package. It all depends on the culture of the firm. In smaller firms, it's often advisable to give equity positions to keep high performers committed for the long term. In some situations, a hybrid profit sharing program is most effective. An incentive pay-for-performance ratio is sometimes advisable because it works, but it can have a downside as well if there is too much focus on the numbers rather than building and maintaining long-term relationships. The principle is simple: When growth and wealth are created for the firm, those responsible should be compensated accordingly. When rainmakers do well, so does everyone else. The benefits are clear: better projects and greater opportunities for professional growth.

Questions

1. Who are the potential rainmakers in your firm?
2. How will you train them?
3. How can you use compensation incentives to reward those who produce measurable value?

Building Your Brand

No firm, not even a global titan, is safe from the rigors of competition. The market is in a constant state of flux. The effects of natural disasters (such as hurricanes or earthquakes), political disruption, wide swings in the equities or currency markets, and the advent of new technology can all cause seismic shifts in the market. Clients are constantly seeking new ideas, always looking for the next opportunity. Smart firms cannot afford to rest on their laurels. They are strategic in how they respond to volatility, continually searching for ways to provide more value.

Clients want solutions. They are challenged by the need to expand their facilities, relocate a division, reposition their business or move their organization to the next state. They need a trusting relationship with experts who can help; those who can navigate the gap between today's operating reality and tomorrow's new business paradigms. They are looking for someone who speaks their language and who is familiar with the unique characteristics of their industry. They not only need an architect, engineer, or designer, but they also need also a problem solver who goes beyond conventional thinking.

Quality, cost, and timely delivery are the primary drivers for clients. One of the three usually takes precedence. Architects and engineers should listen carefully to understand clients' priorities and tailor the project delivery systems to meet and exceed those expectations. If speed is the issue, find ways to streamline the design process without sacrificing quality. The designer who is in tune with the value system of the client and who understands the primary drivers of the project will become a true collaborator and innovator.

Technology is changing many of the rules of the game. It offers huge strategic advantages to those who understand its implications. If architects fail to embrace technology, project leadership will inevitably pass to another profession or service provider. Perhaps licensing laws have lulled the profession into thinking that traditional regulations and standards are what define its value. The overall design and construction pie is growing, and yet we can all hear the common complaint that design services are a chronically undervalued commodity. This trend will continue unless the design profession offers a truly innovative approach to project delivery.

Clients value solutions over traditions. Because so many designers have established ways of doing things, they do not always embrace the latest technologies or processes. Hence, fees suffer and market share shrinks. Newer and better approaches are being sought by clients. Designers who understand how to operate in the intersection of design value and business value will become tomorrow's leaders.

Design works in mysterious ways. Celebrate its mystery. Volkswagen made hearts all around the world beat faster when it reintroduced the new Beetle. The clean lines and rounded forms appealed equally to the head and to the heart. Target has transformed its trademark into a "lovemark." Probably no firm is better at blending business value with design value than Apple, with its unique ability to create high-tech products that form an emotional bond with the user. The power of design thinking is palpable — put it into action at your firm.

Questions

1. What is your firm's brand in terms of competence, style, and delivery?

2. How will you avoid being stuck in the past?

3. What's love got to do with it?

OPERATIONS

Laying the Groundwork for Success

Operations is the process of establishing and managing the context within which work can be done efficiently and effectively. Securing space, procuring equipment, hiring the right staff, and crafting office policies are all prerequisites to establishing a productive working environment. Think of operations as process design. Just like marketing, it is an important part of the overall design process. Without top-quality operations, your talent will be underutilized. Establishing the right context is one of the most powerful things that you can do to optimize the time, talent, and productivity of your staff.

Step One: Create a Strategic Plan

At a management retreat a young designer asked, "Just what do we mean when we talk about the strategic business plan?" She went on to say, "I think strategic plans and business plans are used as devices to get our attention, but then we don't know what to do next. This observation triggered a transformative discussion that has since enabled the firm to achieve, according to one national business publication, best-in-class status. The firm made a commitment to provide every employee with a one-page strategic business plan that could be understood and implemented.

The working definition outlined in the document was simple and straightforward: "Our strategic plan determines our purpose, direction, goals, and the mission of the firm. It reminds us of the big picture and makes sure that we will spend our valuable resources — our time and money — where they will yield the greatest return. We will express this in one page for every employee to understand."

Strategic plans should not be mysterious and inaccessible; rather, they should be a catalyst for meaningful discussion about the future of the firm. Condensing the plan into a one-page document provides much needed focus. Here are the key elements to accomplishing a one-page plan:

1. Include the base year plan and the mission statement of the firm in three sentences or less.

2. List specific targets that will be met in measurable terms in the areas of marketing, operations, professional services, and finance over the next three years.

3. Describe the vision of the firm and how the business will be built and managed to achieve that vision.

The one-page strategic plan can be backed up by a detailed document that provides more detail about the processes and procedures that will be used to implement the goals. Should your staff participate in crafting the plan? Absolutely. Not only will they have good ideas for advancing the organization, but they will work harder to support something that they helped to develop. It may be counterintuitive to think a one-page plan can be effective, but often, less is more.

QUESTIONS

1. How will you gather and organize strategic information?

2. How clearly does your strategic business plan determine your purpose, direction, goals, and mission?

3. How is your plan a catalyst for discussion with all levels of the staff?

4. How will you achieve broad-based buy-in among all staff members?

ONE-PAGE STRATEGIC PLAN SUMMARY

What	*Who*	*When*: Year 1	Year 2	Year 3
MARKETING *Getting the Work*	______ ______ ______ ______	• Book ____$ in new work • Set budget at 8% of gross revenue • Integrate healthcare marketing • Initiate PR program	• Book ____$ in new work • Set budget at 7% of gross revenue • Maintain a 6 mo. backlog • National publications, articles, & seminars	• Book ____$ in new work • Set budget at 6% of gross revenue • Integrate education marketing • Maintain a 12 mo. backlog
OPERATIONS *Supporting the Team*	______ ______ ______ ______	• No project losses • Create CAD plan • Create space plan • Reduce OH 5%	• All Projects Profitable • Implement CAD plan • Implement space plan • Reduce OH 5% • Establish parametrics	• All projects run on target • Full CAD operations • Complete space transition • Maintain low overhead • Achieve *super efficiency*
PROFESSIONAL SERVICES *Doing the Work*	______ ______ ______ ______	• Focus on design • Improve CD process-5% • Use CAD on all projects • Develop LA, ID, STR services	• Win design awards • Improve CD process-10% • 100% CAD literacy • Stand-alone services for select projects	• National design recognition • Top-quality CD accuracy & efficiency • 100% Parametrics • Award-winning LA, ID, STR services
FINANCE *Counting the Money*	______ ______ ______ ______	• ____% in annual revenue • 8% Profit • Budget & track all projects • Positive cash flow	• ____% in annual revenue • 12% profit • All projects profitable • ESOP plan	• ____% in annual revenue • 20% Profit • All projects at target • Profit sharing plan

Mission Statement Summary____

____

____

____

Vision Statement____

____

____

____

Strategic Intent Statement____

____

____

____

THE FIRM'S VISION

A firm's vision is a necessity, not a luxury. By vision, we mean the position or status your firm aspires to achieve within a reasonable time frame. In the best firms, the vision is so energizing that it rallies the staff to make exciting things happen. Without it, design firms are susceptible to drift and lack of focus, which too easily leads to confusion and disharmony.

There are many firms with good mission statements that nevertheless lack a discernible vision. A vision is an understandable, credible, attractive future for your firm expressed in simple language. A good vision will remind your staff of what originally motivated them to choose design as a career. At the end of a long, hard week, staff should still feel a strong sense of a purpose and commitment.

Visions inspire enthusiasm, and they reflect the uniqueness of the firm. They clarify purpose and direction. Visions are about change and about innovative new practice models. A vision is not a mission statement. It is not a reflection of today's reality; it is a declaration of the desirable future condition.

Here are 10 warning signs that your firm may be lacking a clear vision:

1. The firm is not as fun to work in as it once was.
2. There is confusion about purpose and priorities.
3. There is inefficiency.
4. There is resentment toward clients or senior management.
5. There are gossip and rumors in the firm.
6. There is absence of a shared sense of purpose.

7. There is high turnover of staff.
8. There is unnecessary risk avoidance.
9. There is loss of market position and competitive reputation.
10. There is a lack of trust and respect among principals and officers.

What can be done to turn this around? Leaders in the firm must establish clear direction and inspire others to buy in. It isn't always easy. There are choices to be made that require managing behavior, providing authentic leadership, and exercising keen business judgment. Here is what we recommend:

1. Objectively assess the strengths and weaknesses of your firm.
2. Objectively assess the strengths and weakness of similar firms in your market.
3. Involve all levels of staff in the visioning process.
4. Involve clients in an outside-in assessment.
5. Explore options and consider contrarian innovation.
6. Don't tear down the present; build on the foundations you already have in place.
7. Ask what business you are really in and then build on existing value propositions.
8. Determine the key values and cultural elements of the firm.
9. Make choices.
10. Package the vision for internal and external audiences.
11. Implement the vision through an action plan.
12. Track the results, share the data, and adjust as needed to maintain momentum.

Some design organizations suffer from a cognitive dissonance or inconsistency among the organization's attitudes, beliefs, and values versus people's actual behavior. If so, the organization is dysfunctional. It will stay that way until the behavior and the vision are brought into alignment. Great designers are never satisfied with the current level of performance. They see the possibilities ahead even in the face of uncertainty.

QUESTIONS

1. What is your vision? Is it fresh and relevant?
2. Do your staff and clients share the vision?
3. What specific steps will you take to implement your firm's vision?

"My firm lost it's vision."

Decrease Waste and Increase Value

This is a transformational time in the design professions. Outmoded operating methods and rapidly shifting external economic factors are challenging the status quo. In this context, ask yourself these questions:

- Will your firm set a new record for gross revenues this year?
- Will your firm set a new benchmark profit this year?
- How will your firm erase bad habits and inefficiencies?

In the same way that antibodies don't work on viruses, confronting change with conventional wisdom is ineffective. What are best-of-class firms doing to get ahead of the curve to bring better value to their clients while at the same time building value in their own firms?

> ***"If an organization is to be transformed, the social architecture should be revamped. New values must replace the old."***
> DESIGN FUTURES COUNCIL

First, they are doing a better job of measuring their own performance. Even though most of us know that success depends on accomplishing the priority work and that investing our time for the greatest return is vitally important, we often don't practice that way.

What can you do to overcome old habits and promote better utilization? Look for answers in the behavior patterns of the staff. Productivity at all levels can be monitored and improved. Firms that objectively measure actual outcomes will inevitably improve their operations. Consider the following attitudes:

- "Our design business is in the business of change. We constantly monitor what is becoming more important to our clients, what is becoming less important, and how we should we allocate our resources most effectively."
- "We recognize that a well-managed firm keeps costs and expenses low. Efficiency means reducing expenses that don't contribute in some way to serving our clients. We are lean and fit and committed to resiliency."
- "Our design firm is about serving our clients and producing good design — not just about making money. Profit is our reward for serving our clients well. Profit is the means and measure of our service but not an end itself."

Honest feedback drives improvement. Firms that use simple scorecards to measure the inputs and outputs — the volume and the value — find that employees will understand how to manage their time better. The firm's culture will take on new and healthier characteristics. Productivity will improve.

Firms that have discovered how to communicate their priorities learn that their success begins to unfold in new ways. They start to aim higher, providing value-added services that improve the client's condition, meet their profit goals, and provide the financial strength to grow the firm's value.

QUESTIONS

1. What are the five most important ways to measure effectiveness?
2. What will you do to keep costs and expenses low in order to lower your break-even cost?
3. What feedback loops will you implement to monitor progress?

LIVE YOUR VISION: THE WELL-DESIGNED OFFICE ENVIRONMENT

When it comes to your office environment, don't just claim that good design is important. Show your clients that you mean what you say by living your values. Your strategic objectives will be greatly strengthened by practicing what you preach. Demonstrate that strong design and innovative organizational methods lead to high performance. Remember that your firm's office environment defines you in the minds of everyone who walks in the door. It's your brand. How you work is who you are.

There is a significant link between workspace design and firm performance. Architects, engineers, industrial designers, and interior designers are visual people, yet many do not work in a well-designed, organized, uncluttered environment. Design professionals mired in clutter will confuse the priorities of the day.

One of the key priorities for design firms is to use their office environment as a model for clients, fellow professionals, and future employees. The result will be enhanced productivity, greater satisfaction, and lower turnover. We also encourage colleges and universities of architecture, engineering, and design to teach organizational skills and discipline in workplace design and operations strategy.

Consider the prospect of attracting new talent to your firm. Employees are looking for a place to believe in:

1. They want a firm where they can feel appreciated, fairly compensated, and recognized for their true talent.
2. They want to work in a firm where they genuinely like their leaders and mentors and where they feel they can learn and grow as professionals.

3. They want to work in a space where they are reminded of why they chose the design profession in the first place. They want to be proud of the design culture and reputation of the firm.

Take a good look at your own office environment. Now more than ever, architects, engineers, and designers should work in spaces that reflect their values and aspirations. It's not just about what's innovative — it's about what really works. It's not just about the "wow" factor — it's about what people will respect and admire over time.

Sometimes firms are so caught up in day-to-day pressures that they fail to take proper care of their own space. Clutter develops and the organization slips. Living good design is a powerful message to staff and clients alike.

In today's business environment, design firms can't afford not to have an attractive, well-functioning workspace. It's one of the bottom-line factors that future employees consider when choosing which firm to join. It's increasingly influential in client decisions as well. Think of your space as a strategic weapon. Use it wisely. Invest in a well-designed workspace, and expect a return on your investment. You won't be disappointed.

Questions

1. What does your workspace say about your firm? How do you know?
2. How can your office environment be designed to attract new hires and clients?
3. What will you do to create a high-performance workplace for your firm?

Information Overload: Beat the Communications Crunch

What is the single most important factor in producing a successful project? Contrary to popular wisdom, it's not great design, or technology, or management of the budget or schedule. It's communication. Today's complex projects require large teams of professionals that involve the work of many stakeholders, including clients, consultants, and contractors. However, all this expertise is of little use unless it is properly aligned and effectively focused on producing the best results.

Communication is the gravitational field that keeps projects cohesive. Pervasive but invisible, felt but not seen, gravity is what holds the solar system together. People often complain that there is not enough communication on a project, but sometimes there can be too much. Voice mail, email, faxes, cell phones, tweets, texting, pagers, and teleconferencing have altered the communications landscape forever. Ironically, the problem is that there is no longer any conceivable excuse for being out of touch. Yet even with these myriad communications channels, there seems to be more confusion than ever. How is it possible to make sense of information overload and boil it down to simple and effective communication, particularly when so many people are in constant motion?

The core issue is one of signal vs. noise. Not every fax, phone call, or email has the same intrinsic value. Some need immediate attention; others can be put off or should be ignored entirely. Some are important but routine, and administrative staff can handle them. Then there are the critical items that can affect the outcome of a project. This is where judgment comes in. Should that phone call from the contractor be returned right away, or will it hold for a few more hours, days, or even weeks?

The general rule of thumb is that most problems start small and expand quickly if left unattended. Fix them right away, and they're gone, but ignore them at your peril. The good news is that if the problems are small, they can often be delegated to others. Good communicators know which valves to open and close so that information flows effectively to the right places.

The trick is to get the proper linkage between the sender and the receiver. It's important to remember that hearing is not the same thing as listening, and that talking is not the same as connecting. Only when both the sender and the receiver have arrived at a common understanding has real communication taken place.

Suppose a structural question pops up at a job meeting, and you relay the message to your structural engineer by voice mail. You assume things will get taken care of right away. What you don't realize is that the engineer's voice mail already has 10 messages, and he won't get to your call until the end of the day. The contractor, on the other hand, is looking for an answer immediately, and he thinks no one is paying attention.

The contractor sends an email reminder, this time copied to the owner, and the owner follows up by calling you. By this time, you're off at another meeting. Because the owner is involved, you decide to respond in memo form with copies to all three parties plus the project file. Once the paper trail starts, the contractor feels compelled to ask for additional information, and puts the item on the agenda for next week's project meeting.

By this time, the engineer has received the voice mail message and responded to the original question, but only to the contractor. Now another memo is required to reassure everyone that the issue has been satisfactorily put to rest. A simple question that would have originally required five-minute's response time has generated lots of paperwork and more heat than light. The problem has been compounded by the simple but dangerous assumption that access to instant communications means everyone is instantly informed and instantly responsive. That is rarely the case.

By the time you have opened your mail, cleared your phone messages, scanned email, read overnight faxes and memos, and excavated your in-box, you're already buried in information. This bombardment is changing the very nature of the design process. Design cycles are greatly compressed. Much more information flows to all team members simultaneously, and consequently there is less management hierarchy.

What's the best way to cope? There are three basic strategies: sorting, prioritizing, and delegating:

1. **Sorting:** This means dividing up the workflow into discrete chunks, usually on a project-by-project, issue-by-issue basis. When information lands on your desk, you need to know right away where to put it. Some people use multiple in-baskets, one for each project, and this instantly breaks down one big pile of work into digestible pieces. For those who are technically inclined, project management software can be a great help in sorting and tracking information.

2. **Prioritizing:** Obviously, some issues are urgent and demand immediate attention. However, that attention does not always have to come from you. Remember that there are two kinds of priorities: things that are most important and things that have to be done first. They are not always the same. When setting priorities, ask yourself who in your organization or project team is the most appropriate person to handle a particular issue, and then try to think of someone other than yourself. People outside your own office, including consultants, the contractor, and even the client, are fair game. The bigger the group, the more likely it is that someone can get the right answer sooner than you can. Learn how to take advantage of this.

3. **Delegating:** Getting other people to help out is good strategy. It not only reduces your workload, but it also creates buy-in for the solution, spreads knowledge throughout the project team, and demonstrates bench depth to your clients. Just about anyone in your organization can be a problem solver and handle certain tasks effectively. One of the best ways to get this process started is to use junior staff to double check routine information such as which drawings were sent out, which invoices received, and confirming meeting arrangements. Get people started early in understanding the importance of both accepting and delegating tasks. However, always remember that you can delegate authority but not responsibility. At the end of the day, you are still on the hook for the final results — and this is all the more reason to learn how to be a truly effective delegator.

There are other ways to cope with communications overload. Some people like to get to the office early to get at least one uninterrupted hour per day for maximum productivity. Others prefer to leave early but take the office with them by setting up email, voice mail, copying, and faxing at a home office. This enables work to be done in short, quick bursts when it's more convenient.

Still another technique is to limit access to you deliberately. Inform clients that you are generally available for calls at certain hours of the day but less accessible at other times. Turn off your cell phone except when you want to receive calls. Ask consultants and contractors to use email, which is easily scanned, and have an associate or assistant carefully monitor your calls. Software is available that will automatically combine all communications channels so that you can better control the flow.

Information overload is here to stay, and that's both good news and bad. Although it is hardly a new phenomenon, many people have not yet learned how to cope. You might feel like a victim, but you are also a perpetrator. You are receiving much more information than ever before, but you are also sending it out at a record pace. Edit your own communications to focus on the essentials. Do you really need to copy 10 people on that next email? Do your memos have to be longer than one paragraph? Do only what you have to do, and delegate the rest. In other words, generate signal, not noise.

The mark of a good communicator is the ability to make maximum impact with minimum fuss. Ultimately, it's not so much the quantity of communication that matters, it's the quality.

Questions

1. How will you prioritize your communications?
2. Are you a good delegator? Would your staff agree?
3. Do you generate more signal than noise?

"You know, there are better ways to manage a design team."

Designing a Performance Community

Most firms have an abundant supply of brainpower — yet they do not take full advantage of it. Every firm develops networks that operate both inside and outside the organization. These networks don't show up on any chart. Yet the nervous system of the organization behaves differently due to their presence. Morale, performance, humor, and culture are all part of the mix. Firm leaders need to become more involved in understanding and interweaving their processes and systems with the informal networks; managing network power is a significant strategic issue for firms.

For example, when there is a strong sense of community, existing employees are inclined to bring in new like-minded talent, and the firm becomes more magnetic in how it attracts talent. There is lower turnover and more peer accountability.

> ***"The root of most conflicts and misunderstandings lies in the absence of communications."***
> JAMES BARKSDALE

Designing a performance-based firm is an achievable goal. This is a firm that consistently delivers results. One way to get started is to establish a business model (including the values and vision of the firm) that people understand and respect. Here are some steps to creating a performance-based community in your organization:

- Establish strategic clarity. What do you stand for and how are you organized achieve it? This becomes your brand promise.
- Respect the dignity of all, especially those who need guidance on performance issues.

- Treat all people fairly — nothing reveals the character of leadership more transparently.
- Be open about financial objectives and performance.
- Measure what you value because you will become what you measure.

What works inside a firm gets translated externally as well. Your network power will determine how you keep and attract both the best clients and the best talent.

To optimize daily performance, break away from old limiting beliefs and habit patterns, and get rid of background noise:

1. Spend time with people you want to be like; you are likely to become more like them.
2. Establish eye contact with and smile frequently at others.
3. Confront and deal with situations involving conflict early on.
4. Don't think in black and white terms.
5. Don't associate with toxic people.

Your role in strengthening the firm requires both thought and action. Successful firms are led by people who understand this and who can exercise them daily.

Questions

1. How would your staff describe your personality?
2. How will you develop a sense of community in your firm?
3. How will you improve the social networks in your organization?

HANDING OFF: DELEGATION BY DESIGN

In our increasingly complex world, no single entity has the talent, knowledge, experience, or resources to produce a project entirely alone. Project success hinges on the choreography among the owner, architect, engineer, consultant, contractor, suppliers, and subcontractors. This means that there is real opportunity for people who know how to get the best out of a group effort, respecting the contributions of individual talents while bending those talents to the overall good of the project. While it takes individual talent to produce good results, teamwork is always more powerful.

As team members, we assume that we understand what is required, and we do our best to make it happen. But things don't always turn out the way we expect. We depend on others for information to do our part, and we delegate work to the team so that they can do theirs. Trouble festers if there is a glitch at either end of the transaction.

A classic example is the transition between the construction documents (CD) and construction administration (CA) phases of a project. Many good intentions have gone up in smoke during CA, not to mention profits, because the design and budget are not reconciled or there is insufficient fee remaining to complete the job properly. It is only during the CA period that the true quality and value of the designer's work are made manifest, where the project gets translated from mere lines on paper to actual built space. Without good CA, the best design intentions come to naught. This is where the absence of a good hand-off can have a huge impact on the outcome.

The fundamentals of communication are simple to understand but surprisingly difficult to implement. Pay attention to your hand-offs. Be a good "customer" by not accepting hand-offs that are incomplete, confusing, or just plain wrong. Be a good "supplier" by making sure you know what the next person in line is really dealing with and what he or she needs to get the job done.

The role of a project manager represents real value added to the design process, where the cost of making decisions and choreographing players in the project often go unrecognized and unappreciated. In a very real sense, design is about being in the leadership business.

QUESTIONS

1. What's your delegation style?
2. How will you use your position to help staff feel understood and connected?
3. How will you teach your staff to delegate properly?

Scale is Strategic

Visionary design leaders understand that growth is a strategic advantage. Some principals operate their firms on a steady-state basis without any urgent desire to grow. Content with the status quo, they simply don't think of it. But the most successful firms are focused on growth. Some even make it policy. They do this because they have discovered that size matters. Grow quickly or you will be overtaken and lose your competitive edge. Growth is a strategic advantage because:

1. It better serves growing clients.
2. It improves shareholder value.
3. It provides opportunities for staff development and career building.
4. It provides increased capacity to deliver the goods.

Growth begins as an attitude. Smart firm leaders know that they cannot grow their own firm unless they also contribute to the growth of their clients. The value added is an intelligent investment. Growth improves profitability and the balance sheet — not just staff size, so it pays to make growth a policy. Some firms are establishing a market-centered model of growth. Consider these components:

1. Each market center is established as a profit center. Most firms set a 10 percent to 15 percent profit margin as a target.
2. Each market center acts as a central bank of expert knowledge — the most up-to-date storehouse of information about their service areas.

3. Each market center is led by an energetic performer who knows how to get results and can achieve the growth necessary to meet the firm's plan.

Growth can be measured in many ways, including staff size, revenues, service offerings, and specialty markets. One key growth area is in the quality of project management. Importantly, this also indicates how consistently profitable that growth is.

> ***"It is not the strongest of the species that survive, nor the most intelligent, but the one most responsive to change."***
> CHARLES DARWIN

QUESTIONS

1. How will you grow to improve shareholder value and provide opportunities for staff development?
2. Your firm cannot grow unless you contribute to the growth of your clients. What are you doing for them?
3. Growth is not just in size. It is multi-dimensional. What is your definition of growth?

Growth by Design

Perhaps you're lucky and the firm is busy, backlog is up, and revenue projections are looking strong. Feeling good? Not so fast! When your biggest problem is finding enough qualified people to staff your projects, you are in the danger zone called growth.

It might feel terrific to have a list of clients eager for your attention, but if growth is not carefully managed, big problems can result. It is ironic but true that firms suffer more long-term damage from poorly managed growth than from lack of work. This is because when work is thin, it is much easier to focus on exactly what needs to be done in order to survive. But when times are flush, problems are easily camouflaged, and they will surprise you at the most unexpected and inopportune times. Remember that the damage done by a project gone sour can last for years (and sometimes forever in the mind of the client).

For many firms, growth is reactive — people don't think about why, how, or when to grow until they are overcome by pressing deadlines. Sometimes that long-awaited project that has been on hold finally gets the green light. Sometimes a long-shot proposal or design competition hits pay dirt. Sometimes a client decides to increase the scope of work without adjusting the schedule.

A few new jobs in the office can put unexpected pressure on other obligations. The common reaction is to hire more staff as quickly as possible. But don't do anything until you have thought through the strategy, tactics, and logistics of managing growth properly.

Managing growth is not about putting warm bodies in empty chairs and hoping for the best. Adding staff always causes a revenue squeeze and can lead to quality control problems. First, you have to take time out of your already busy schedule to sort through resumes and check references, conduct interviews, get feedback from colleagues, structure an offer, confirm an entry date, and arrange the proper support and resources for the new hires.

When the new staff arrives, you are likewise distracted by the usual meeting and greeting, orientation on standard policies and protocols, and the extra dose of project supervision required to ensure a smooth transition.

> ***"The best way to get a good idea is to get a lot of ideas."***
> LINUS PAULING

Multiply all of this by the number of new staff you need, and you can easily see that when you are in a recruiting blitz, nothing else going on in the firm will get the usual measure of attention. On top of all this, the new staff will be collecting a paycheck at least 30 to 60 days before invoices for their work will be paid by the client, so you are financing all this growth up front.

The good news is that the pressure for growth will force you to think more strategically about your business and the clients you serve. It will make you reconsider your ideal staffing profile, what kinds of talent you need, who your real contributors are, the nature of your compensation structure, and how your firm stacks up against the competition as a desirable place to work.

The very best time to do this thinking is before you need new people. This is important for two reasons: It reduces pressure when you really need to concentrate on current deadlines, and it impresses your staff as well as prospective hires, who are now persuaded that you do, in fact, think ahead of the curve. The truth is that smart firms are always in recruiting mode, seeking the best-qualified talent whether or not they are in hiring mode. There is a world of difference between the two.

When opportunity knocks and you have to hire quickly, what's the best way to go about it?

1. **Be sensitive not only to the short-term pressure for extra staff but to the longer-term implications.** When today's fire drill is over, where will your new staff be assigned next? To be successful, you need to be resilient, and this means that your marketing strategy and your staffing plan have to be synchronized. As you hire, make sure that the current growth spurt will be sustainable.

2. **Review and refresh your employee manual, compensation package, office policies, and orientation program.** If you don't have an orientation program, then create one, and make sure that everyone in the firm goes through it, both recent and longer-term employees. Remember that you want the new staff to hit the ground running, and the key to making this happen is not just the new staff themselves (who are already eager to adapt) but also the existing staff who have to adapt to all those new hires. Be prepared for some resistance to the new people; it's human nature. Smooth this transition by organizing some social events that allow new staff to soak up the corporate culture in a less formal setting while presenting an opportunity for existing staff to get to know their new coworkers.

3. **On the logistics side, make sure that adequate technology is in place to support additional workload.** As the firm grows, you will need to plan for additional capacity in work space, phone lines, fax machines, printers, server capacity, administrative help, and filing space. Are your computers, networks, and software licenses up to date? Nothing is worse than getting a new person on board without their requisite tools being effective from day one, but it happens surprisingly often. Remember that the first day on the job makes a powerful impression on new staff — your organization and preparation set the tone for their future success.

When you have done all of this, the real job of smart growth is just beginning. New staff need extra coaching. Make time to check in every couple of days to see how things are going. Ask them what's working well and what still needs some attention. Listen carefully to their observations about the firm because these fresh impressions are extremely valuable. Make sure that you take the steps that will support their success, and at the same time stay alert for signs that the fit might not be right. And if it's not right, end the association as soon as possible regardless of looming deadlines.

The single biggest danger from unstructured, unplanned, and unmanaged growth is the threat to quality control. It is very easy for new staff to make mistakes — not because they are ignorant or unskilled but because they are unfamiliar with your system. If mistakes are made, don't compound them by blaming the new people: Most likely the fault lies with management who failed to give proper direction in the first place. Quality control is the single biggest risk factor during rapid growth. (The second is protecting your cash flow.)

Your hiring decisions determine your demographics. Since people are the core of your enterprise, you are literally shaping the personality of the organization. Hire with a long-term strategy in mind. Don't just react to today's deadlines or temporary market pressures. Even if you have to move fast, you can still make the right moves.

Questions

1. How do you manage growth? When do you know it's needed?

2. What is your staffing profile and the types of people you need?

3. How is your growth sustainable?

Leveraging Generational Differences

The baby boom has had a profound effect on the economy, the environment, and social values. If you manage a design firm today, the odds are pretty good that you are a baby boomer. You have come of age in the most prosperous and technologically advanced generation in history. Until, that is, the arrival of Generation X, Generation Y, and the Millenials.

It should come as no surprise that various generations behave differently. People who grow up in different times and under different influences develop different values. This is a reflection of progress. Current events for one generation are history to the next.

The differences between generations can be both subtle and profound, including attitudes toward dress, speech, lifestyle, social customs, the work ethic, and even music. A lot has been written recently about Generation X, and not all of it is flattering. Adjectives such as lazy, self-absorbed, and greedy have been used, but be cautious about believing everything you read. Instead, deal with your staff as people, not as labels. They may be part of a generational cohort, but each is an individual.

In managing your design firm, you may notice some chafing among individuals or groups of different ages. Different personal or educational backgrounds, levels of experience, and expectations about work/life balance and compensation all contribute to this. Be alert but not alarmed. If properly dealt with, this diversity can be very positive for an organization as long as you handle it in a straightforward manner. Diversity can be delightful, and it makes for a stronger firm. However, do not allow these differences to become dissension. Multi-generational firms can make good use of several generations on project teams to help break down inherent boundaries.

When dealing with generational differences, minimize the negatives and exploit the positives. What is it that attracts people to work at your firm? What gets them excited? What special complementary skills does the firm need to be successful? How can each generation learn from the other? Remember that there are bright and committed people of all ages. Your job as a manager is to clearly communicate the vision and mission of the organization so that all of the staff pulls together. This is called leadership.

A number of years ago, a firm in the Midwest provided an example. This firm had not yet entered the computer age. It was clear that a transition to more sophisticated technology was needed, but there was considerable resistance from the older generation, who were already not particularly computer savvy or interested in "Nintendo architecture."

The younger staff, however, was energized and excited about using the new technology. Rather than push the changeover from the top down, senior management let it percolate from the bottom up, and in a very short time, computers and project management software became the standard production tools for everyone. Some of the best teachers were the younger staff, and their enthusiasm was infectious. Today, computers are used by everyone in that firm. But what will the next breakthrough be? Don't you want to get in early — and get ahead?

Remember that each and every generation produces its share of leaders. If you are a baby boomer, the odds are pretty good that at one time you were considered cocky, idealistic, impatient, or even weird. Over time, these attributes transformed into confidence, vision, efficiency, and creativity. With your help as a leader and mentor, the next generations that will succeed you will grow and learn. And if you're smart, you'll make a point of learning from them as well.

QUESTIONS

1. How will you deal with your staff as people as opposed to labels, titles, or numbers?
2. How will you exploit the positives of demographic differences?
3. Multi-generational teams can be very effective. How will you create such teams in your firm?

Unlikely conversations among designers.

SUSTAINING GROWTH

When times are busy, the pressure to grow increases. Like any other dynamic change, growth is tricky, and it requires continual attention. Growth is not just a matter of adding headcount. The most important aspect is adding the right kind of staff and integrating them into the firm effectively.

Growth may be the result of short-term pressure such as a major new commission with a tight deadline, or it may be due to a strategic shift such as adding new markets and services or even acquiring or merging with another firm in order to extend market reach. Either way, there are some fundamentals to be reckoned with.

Growth makes all things different. To most people, growth is a sign of success, but it can also produce lots of anxiety, both obvious and latent. Even changes that most of us would consider to be unalloyed good news, such as winning the lottery, have been shown to create significant stress in the lives of those affected.

For the newer staff in the office, there will be pressure both to fit in and to stand out. New arrivals will want to make a good first impression and flex their muscles a bit in order to establish their place in the office hierarchy. On the other hand, they will also need to blend in, learn the ropes, find out how things really get done, and figure out the corporate culture and tribal customs of the new firm. If they don't push a little, they will lose the opportunity to make a positive difference in the new firm and may even unwittingly sabotage their chance for subsequent promotion because first impressions are so powerful. If they stand out too much, there will be resentment from those who have already paid their dues and don't want to see their position in the office pecking order jeopardized.

For the veterans, there is generally a dual reaction to the new faces: relief and added stress. First, of course, is relief that much-needed help is on the way. With new staff, there is more help to get things done, and the pressure for overtime will diminish, or at least be more widely distributed. The appearance of extra resources reassures everyone that senior management understands the situation and is willing to take needed action. At the same time, there is the all too human reaction of *What will this mean for me?* If the new staff is brighter, faster, better trained, or more personable, then subtle conflict can result. It can be mitigated to a certain degree by lots of communication about who was hired and why, what he or she will be expected to contribute, and what kind of help he or she will need from the old guard in order to be successful.

This last point is particularly important because the "old timers" are the ones who are usually relied upon to teach the new recruits what is needed and how to get things done. Any problems with transferring this "office DNA" can cause big problems later if standards are not met or if there is ambiguity or confusion about goals. Thus, it pays to get both sides to understand that they need each other.

The mix of the old and the new in the same organization is similar in some ways to what happens with planetary orbits. The introduction of any new mass — asteroid, moon, or planet — has an immediate and palpable effect on the entire solar system. Gravitationally speaking, each body, whatever its size, shape, or speed, affects all others, even at a great distance. The same effect is true in organizations where the addition of any new staff will have both a project-based as well as firm-wide effect.

The good news, of course, is that when growth is properly planned for and managed, it is sustainable for the long term. The firm gains talent, strength, stature, capacity, and self-confidence. However, if the effects of growth are ignored, relationships will be unexpectedly altered, and there may even be collisions that cause major disruption. Like real gravity, organizational gravity is invisible, but its effects are palpable and everybody feels them in every area of the firm. Bearing this in mind, as you decide to grow your firm, develop an implementation plan. Ask these essential questions:

- Why did you decide to grow?
- What specific benefits do you hope to achieve?
- How much will it cost in terms of salaries, overhead, space, and equipment?
- How long will it take?
- How will growth affect existing staff, clients, and projects?
- Can growth be sustained beyond the immediate short-term need?
- What will the new staff be doing two or three years down the road?

Think of growth management as if you were the dean of admissions at a college whose job it is to compose and balance an entire class of talented and diverse individuals. Since staff is by far the most expensive and most productive asset in any design firm, this is a critical strategic challenge. Don't take it for granted. If you do it right, then you are on your way to an interesting and prosperous future.

Questions

1. How does growth cause stress as well as relief for your firm?
2. What is your plan to create sustainable growth in your firm?
3. How does your point of view about growth contribute to work/life balance in your firm?

COMPLEXITY AND FIRM SIZE

Increasing the size of your firm used to be a sure signal of success. Staff size is often touted by firm leaders as proof that they are getting stronger and healthier. But this is not necessarily so. Here's why: As organizations grow, they undergo structural transitions that differ both in kind and degree. Larger organizations often develop new and unanticipated problems. Sometimes the problems lead to a near collapse before a workable leadership structure is put into place. Anthropologist Robin Dunbar of Great Britain has developed a biology-based theory that sheds light on the issue of organizational growth. According to Dunbar, functional units larger than about 150 people cannot be effectively managed, nor can their members build critical bonds of support, loyalty, and a sense of mutual reliability. Dunbar's work suggests that group size is a key management issue for design managers.

The figure of 150 seems to represent the maximum number of individuals with whom we can have a genuine social relationship — the kind of relationship that goes with knowing who the people are and how they relate to each other. Microsoft keeps business units to a 200-person maximum, a limit that allows most people to know each other by name and enables tracking of their contributions within the accountability structure. Many professional firms limit their studio size to 12 to 20 people.

Here are some recommendations for optimal size, span of control, and business group performance:

- **Optimum retreat size:** 7.
  Provides the most effective communication and bonding.
- **Maximum retreat size:** 17
  Acceptable levels of communication and bonding are still possible.

....

- **Optimum span of control:** 30
  Provides for both individual and group needs.
- **Maximum span of control:** 65
  Acceptable individual and group needs are possible.

....

- **Optimum practice size for team performance:** 18
  Provides for an effective performance community.
- **Maximum practice size for team performance:** 150
  Acceptable performance community is possible.

Highly capable leaders may stretch the performance of these numbers, but not by much. Functional units of larger than 150 people cannot be effectively managed nor can their members build critical bonds of support, loyalty, and a sense of confident mutual reliability.

QUESTIONS

1. What are the current sizes of your teams, studios, and working groups?
2. How do you determine the maximum number of people that can form a team?
3. What size organization is most productive for you?

Choosing Your Leaders

A firm in the South decided that it was time to promote several younger associates. The principals agreed that the time was right, but they disagreed on who, why, and how. This is often the case in growing firms. Regrettably but not surprisingly, a balanced and critical assessment of talent within firms is among the most poorly performed processes.

Above all, consideration for promotion requires demonstrated leadership, and underlying this is respect within the organization. In professional firms, respect is earned in various ways. We look for sound decision making, the ability to admit mistakes, assuming accountability in day-to-day behavior, and prioritizing the client's best interest ahead of personal ego or agenda.

In the firm noted above, three younger associates were evaluated and then elevated to new levels of responsibility in the firm. During the process, the older partners earned one another's respect for giving the process thoughtful review. The rest of the staff also better understood how day-to-day choices, behaviors, and character affect both the promotion prospects and actions of the leaders. No leader can break trust with his firm's staff and expect to keep influencing them. Just as in client relationships, trust is the foundation of leadership.

Questions

1. How do you promote from within?
2. What is your leadership transition plan?
3. Who is respected for true leadership skills in your organization? Why?

LEADERSHIP STRENGTH ASSESSMENT

Partner Evaluation

1. Challenging processes—Continuing improvements
2. Vision clarity—ability to inspire others
3. Systematic priority planning, enabling others to succeed
4. Role model—Stature in field
5. Boosts morale especially during times of stress
6. Builds financial resource strength
7. Communications are at exemplary levels

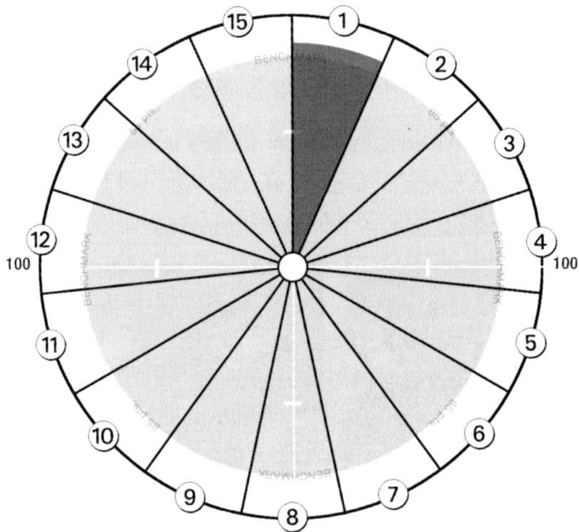

8. Collaborative spirit enriching the people and organizations
9. Steady and strong without alienating egotistic pride
10. Work ethic without micromanagement
11. Applied brilliance—Intellectual power
12. Builds rapport, respect, admiration
13. Custom to Firm's Core Values/Culture
14. Custom to Firm's Core Values/Culture
15. Custom to Firm's Core Values/Culture

Delivering Bad News

People sometimes find themselves facing unpleasant surprises. And all too often the bad news comes in clusters. It may be a star member of the staff who abruptly leaves, it may be a liability claim that comes out of nowhere, or it may be an unexpected budget problem on a project.

Budget crises, staffing problems, quality complaints, and liability surprises are all too common. Even if it's not your fault, it's on your turf, and somebody needs to restore equilibrium.

Don't get discouraged. Remember that problem-solving is what reveals the true character of the people involved. To stay on top of the game, successful firms should anticipate that really bad news most certainly will crop up sometime. Knowing how to process bad news can become a strategic strength for your organization. When the tough situations occur, remember that they are an opportunity for you to provide solutions.

You can set yourself apart from those who insist on acting in ways that reinforce the negatives. When there is bad news, don't attempt to hide it. As quickly as possible, face up to the situation and put an affirmative plan into action that informs all the stakeholders. Your message should be factual, clear, and forthright about the problem at hand.

Most important, you should specify next steps: Who is going to what and by when? Communicating the bad news is a basic professional responsibility, but it is moving forward with options and solutions that is even more important and makes for true professionalism. While bad news may test the character of the firm, it need not weaken the organization or its relationships. How a firm works under pressure in times of crisis will, in fact, define its character.

QUESTIONS

1. How do you deliver bad news?

2. How will you anticipate better?

3. How will you put actions to your ideas?

"Ve vill need bigger crystal ball-
I see enormous opportunities ahead,"

Leading Indicators of Organizational Health

Management gurus are fond of saying that in order to manage something, it must first be measured. Measurement requires both data and calibration. However, information and wisdom are not the same thing; collecting data and knowing what to do with it are entirely different skill sets.

There is usually a great deal of resistance in the design profession about measuring creativity, as if quantifying design somehow undercuts its value. Ironically, the opposite is true. It is the very lack of measurement that causes so much confusion in the eyes of our clients about the value of what we do.

How does good design contribute to client success? How is this value produced? How can the design process, and thereby the results, be greatly improved? The answers to these fundamental questions form the basis for finding the sweet spot between creative design and profitability.

> ***"If we did all the things we are capable of doing, we would literally astonish ourselves."***
> THOMAS EDISON

There are numerous software packages that will track key indicators for a project or an entire firm. The printouts abound, and they make our eyes glaze over. We can dig deep into details and pull out arcane bits of data, but do we really understand what this data is telling us and, moreover, what to do about it? Probably not, because we often suffer from too much data or data that is poorly organized.

A printout presents a frozen slice of life at a specific point in time. Yet we know that all clients, projects, staff, and firms are dynamic in nature and constantly changing. By the time we get our hands on the numbers, the problem has already occurred, and it's often too late to fix, or the nature of the problem has changed. We need a way to digest the data without being overwhelmed. What's to be done?

Start by simplifying. Make sure that the data you receive is really data, not information contaminated by opinion. (A classic example is the percent complete column on a project management summary, which implies a soothing precision that is simply not possible to achieve.) When you have separated fact from opinion, you have taken the first step. Now condense and arrange the information to illustrate not only the status of the situation but also trends. It is possible to do a quick and accurate scan by looking at only six key indicators:

1. **Monthly billings.** Cash flow is the lifeblood of a design firm, and presumably you are already aware of how much cash is needed to sustain your organization for a typical month's operation. If the accounting department does not send out invoices for at least that amount every month, then eventually you'll be in trouble. Therefore, the first and most important number is the dollar amount of monthly billings. While this may ebb and flow a bit, don't let the three-month blended average fall below target. Benchmark target: 8.5 percent of your annual revenue should be billed every month on average.

2. **Accounts receivable.** Billing your clients is one thing, getting paid is another. A/R measures the average number of days required for collection. Obviously, quicker is better. There is no cardinal rule that says you have to wait 30 days before billing a project. Customize your billing cycles for each individual client so that your invoices can be approved and paid as quickly as possible based on their accounting practices. An A/R report that begins to show a delay in

collections could signal an unhappy client or an unresolved problem. Benchmark target: 45 days or better for A/R.

3. **Staff utilization ratio.** Your staff is your most valuable and expensive asset — make sure it's being used to full advantage. Staff utilization is the ratio of billable hours divided by the total hours for all staff. There will always be some non-billable time for vacation, sick days, holidays, administration, and marketing, but you want to keep the utilization ratio as high as possible — it's akin to your batting average. It doesn't hurt to let your staff know how many billable hours you expect them to produce each month. But beware — being busy is not the same thing as being productive. Benchmark target: a minimum of 70 percent for staff utilization.

4. **Backlog.** This is your unburned fee — the amount of fee remaining in a project at any given time. Track backlog for all projects and keep a running total. This will translate pretty well into a staffing projection. If you see a bump in your backlog, you may be in a hiring mode; if you see a dip, you'll either have to increase your marketing effort or downsize. Backlog is the amount of fuel in the tank. Benchmark target: maintain a minimum of six months of backlog at all times.

5. **Marketing report.** You can't do the work unless you bring it in first. Therefore, keep track of your new booked work every month and measure progress against an annual goal. New booked work comes in two flavors: entirely new work and additional services on existing projects. Track both. And make sure that the new booked work is real, which means it has a written commitment from the client that the project has been authorized to proceed. As with monthly billings, new booked work is somewhat episodic, so pay attention to the three-month rolling average. And remember

that projects are often delayed or canceled, which means that new booked work is not the same thing as future revenue. Benchmark target: 8.5 percent or more of annual gross billings should be booked each month.

6. **Profitability.** Profits are essential to a healthy firm, enabling you to acquire the best technology and attract the best people. Structure your organization so that profits are accrued on a monthly basis and log the cumulative total. Think of profit like rent; as a bill that must be paid every month. This technique practically guarantees a black bottom line every year. Benchmark target: a minimum profit margin of 10 percent with a goal of 15 percent.

By keeping track of these six indicators, all of which are quantitative, not qualitative, you'll be able to develop a quick and accurate sense of what's going on in your firm, where the problems are, and what needs attention. All this data is readily available from standard financial reports and is easily formatted on a single sheet of paper.

These six data points are like the gauges on a dashboard: They won't steer the bus for you, but they will enable you to be a much better driver. By developing management techniques that reduce complexity and confusion in your practice — techniques that everyone can understand — you'll free up valuable time for doing the single most important thing you do — top quality design.

Questions

1. What data will you measure and manage each month?
2. How will you ensure that the data is objective?
3. How will you use the six key indicators? Are there others?

Performance-Based Incentives: Motivating Your Firm

The closing of each year's books is a good time for strategic thinking about the year to come. It's a great time to ask the tough questions, make adjustments, and set expectations. The opportunity for a fresh start finds us returning to one particular issue time and again: What's really driving performance in the organization?

Many client firms with which we've worked have expressed concerns about maintaining consistently high standards in the work they produce and the relationships they maintain.

Motivating staff to continually strive for excellence is difficult. The two fundamentals of maintaining it are a clearly articulated code of professional ethics and a well-considered performance-based compensation plan. When implemented strategically, they will lead to heightened levels of profitability, productivity, and professional satisfaction.

> ***"Create the culture that will give your staff the crucial feeling that they are singly important and making a difference."***
>
> JONAS SALK

Nearly a third of firms have reported experiencing dissatisfaction with their incentive plans or are uncertain if their plans actually have a significant impact on overall organizational performance.

With this in mind, we have devised a checklist of characteristics to be included when creating a performance-based incentive program for your firm. Experience has shown that it should be inclusive, motivational, and well-defined. Such a program has the potential to be a powerful motivator, enhancing both productivity and profitability. The five key components of an effective plan are:

- Aim for incentives that pay at least 15 percent of base salary.
- Key personnel benefiting from the incentive program usually include principals, department heads, project managers and top management rather than hourly employees.
- Key performance metrics include a blend of overall firm profitability, the performance of specific profit centers, and individual performance.
- The plan's criteria should be clearly communicated and recognize the top performers in objective ways.
- Focus on rewarding behavior, outcomes, activities, and accomplishments that significantly contribute to the firm's effectiveness and profitability.

QUESTIONS

1. What performance-based compensation plan will work in your firm?
2. How will this plan make your firm more profitable?
3. What are you willing to invest in order to create a culture of excellence?

BEWARE "LOS"

When a spacecraft returns from orbit, there is about a four-minute period when the buildup of electromagnetic interference is sufficient to block out all radio contact. During this period, no communication is possible between the spacecraft and ground control. At NASA, this period is officially known as "LOS" or "loss of signal."

A similar kind of LOS occurs between senior management and staff. Whether you realize it or not, most organizations comprise layers of management that too often operate like a caste system. Horizontal communication in any given layer is relatively easy and fluid, but communication either up or down the ladder is not. (Think of an apartment or condo building; it's much more likely that you'll be friendly with a neighbor down the hall than one three floors up even though everyone uses the same elevator.) At the highest level, all communication with senior management from below is filtered in some important way. Whether this editing is conscious or unconscious, it is ubiquitous. The chief executive almost never gets the straight scoop: He or she gets an edited version that is packaged for personal consumption. *Here is what we want the boss to know* or *Here is what we think the boss should know* are the filters. Because the staff sees the boss differently than the boss views himself or herself, the view from the bridge is always a bit foggy, with the consequence that senior management is usually somewhat out of touch with the rank and file.

Obviously, any firm whose synapses are clogged with too much filtering cannot operate nimbly, effectively, or collaboratively. To combat the phenomenon of LOS, it's very important to establish a communication culture that encourages candor. Straight talk, clear thinking, and effectiveness go hand in hand.

One good way to do this is to set up project teams that include staff from several different layers in the organization. Such cross-functional teams are a good way to break down the inherent barriers caused by management hierarchies. Another good tactic is to conduct periodic 360-degree staff reviews, in which each staff member is reviewed not just by superiors but peers and subordinates as well. This helps everyone understand how they come across to others in the organization, whatever their position.

Still another strategy is to promote from within whenever possible. If the ranks of senior management are substantially filled with those who worked their way up from the trenches, it will be easier to maintain trust in senior management.

Most important, the chief executive officer must set the right tone. If the communication style is one of openness and approachability, this will be imitated by the rest of the organization. If, on the other hand, the chief executive is remote, guarded, and hard to read, the rest of the staff will conduct itself accordingly.

When considering your communication style, remember that broadcasting and receiving are not the same thing. Too often what we say is totally misinterpreted by the audience, despite the best intentions. It's like speaking French to an audience of Germans: No matter how fluent you are, you're bound to be misunderstood. To be a better communicator, it's very important to check with your audience about what they heard, not what you said. You'll be amazed at the difference.

As the leader, the burden falls on you to ensure that you are both sending and receiving information in the right way — clearly, succinctly, and accurately. Communication is the neural network of your firm; nothing gets done without it. When you are in a position of authority, it's too easy and seductive to preach from your pulpit and assume that you are being listened to and understood (much less followed). It's much tougher and much more important to be a good listener. Good listeners readily absorb information and ideas, and engender trust, which is how they become influential in the first place.

All firms and organizations have LOS to some degree. When you are the leader of a firm, you are especially susceptible to its symptoms. To get the best out of your staff, they need to know how to reach you. Give them the means and the methods, and you will surprised by the results.

QUESTIONS

1. What are the symptoms of LOS in your firm?
2. What will you do to reduce your LOS?
3. How will you become a better listener?

Risky Business

Big Improvements Come From Managing Rather Than Avoiding Risk

"Risk" is a much-misunderstood word in the A/E/C industry. It is generally viewed as a negative, something to be avoided at all cost. While risk is defined as exposure to possible loss or injury, this does not necessarily mean that the bad stuff will happen. In fact, it rarely does (which is what keeps insurance companies in business). Another way of thinking about risk is that it's a condition that requires an extra measure of attention in order to achieve the desired outcome. In this sense, if risk is embraced and managed rather than delegated or avoided, the odds of success increase considerably.

Risk is sometimes confused with unpredictability, a related but quite different condition. Things that are unpredictable are not necessarily risky, and vice versa. For example, skydiving may be risky, but it is predictable because you know exactly what will happen when you jump out of a plane: Gravity takes over. On the other hand, next year's inflation rate may be unpredictable, but it is not risky: You can choose to lock in today's prices with purchasing agreements for future delivery.

In the A/E/C industry, the concept of risk avoidance is deeply embedded in standard contract language. In fact, the amount of text devoted to risk, liability, insurance requirements, and punitive damages greatly outweighs the language devoted to the basic value proposition of the project (schematic design and design development). Contractually speaking, we are far more concerned about what to avoid than what we are striving to achieve, which is exactly backward. Too much focus on risk avoidance tends to drive a wedge between key members of the project team and often leads to defensive rather than collaborative behavior. This is because traditional contracts assign risk to specific participants rather than to the team as a whole. By accepting individual risk, team members become targets for blame and are motivated to look after their own interests first, whereas with shared risk, the overall team performance is what matters most, and this changes the dynamics considerably.

Managing Risk

Fortunately, with a few fundamental changes, managing the inherent risk of designing, documenting, and delivering buildings can be dramatically improved. In the process, it will be possible to produce better designed, better built projects at less cost. How will this happen?

Let's start with the owner, who carries the most responsibility and hence the most exposure. There are five generic kinds of risk with which owners must contend: scope, cost, schedule, quality, and what can be called unpredictable disruptive events (accidents, bad weather, natural disasters, labor strikes, supply chain problems, etc.).

Because the owner is in a position to determine the scope of work in advance, it would seem that there should be relatively little risk in that regard. However, scope creep is a frequent occurrence; it's probably the most common cause of blown budgets and schedules. Project scope can increase for unanticipated reasons (such as hidden conditions uncovered during a renovation project that require additional work), but such instances can be largely avoided with sufficient due diligence before the job is undertaken. With proper research, there is really no reason to be surprised.

Scope increases due to user group interaction are another matter but, once again, well under the control of a competent owner. If proper programming is done before the final project scope is approved, then subsequent changes can be minimized if not eliminated entirely. This requires buy-in from the affected stakeholders, of course. Problems occur if owners bend to internal pressure for changes after the project is underway. When this happens, every proposed deviation from the original approved scope should be assessed for the impact on schedule and budget before being implemented. Once again, there's no reason for anyone to get caught off guard; all that's required is to pay attention.

Cost control is probably the biggest risk that owners face. In an attempt to mitigate this risk, owners attempt to shift it to architects (by insisting that any redesign needed to comply with the budget be done at no cost to the owner) or the contractor (by requiring a fixed-price bid). The result is that owners give up a large measure of control, which has the unintended consequence of actually increasing the likelihood of suboptimal results.

All fixed-price bids include a layer of fat, also known as contingency, which is added to the base price for labor and materials. Therefore, the bid price is never the lowest possible price. The owner agrees to absorb the contingency in order to avoid the risk of price increases down the road, essentially paying in advance for something that might not happen. However, fixed-price bidding is no guarantee against future price increases because it invites change orders.

By requiring a fixed-price bid, the owner is basically daring the contractor to make a bet about market fluctuations over the life of the project. Even worse, by waiting until the construction documents are completed to solicit the bids, owners don't find out until it's too late what the actual cost of the project will be. If the numbers are not favorable, then value engineering ensues and project scope and quality will suffer.

A better and less risky way of managing cost is to price the job on a continuous basis as design proceeds, using both benchmarking and real-time market data. This takes the mystery out of money. Computer programs can accurately track quantities, and real-time costs for labor and materials can be easily checked on the Internet. Continuous tracking of cost reduces the need for a hefty contingency because purchasing agreements can be put into place that lock in current prices for a specified future delivery date. This benefits not only the owner (who will pay less) but also suppliers (who can plan their production more efficiently, thus keeping costs down).

While competitive bidding is often viewed by owners as the best (and only) way to get the lowest possible price, it actually has the opposite effect. The bid price is almost never the final price. Once the envelopes are opened, scoping sessions are conducted to review and verify the details: This is just negotiation by another name. With continuous cost review, this poker game can be avoided, with the added benefit of eliminating the need for redesign, saving additional time and money as well as protecting project scope and quality.

Now let's turn our attention to the schedule. Most complex projects are a multi-year adventure, requiring the participation of dozens of architects, engineers, consultants, suppliers, and subcontractors. It's relatively easy to create a bar chart that neatly projects the precise start and finish dates of the various phases and sub-tasks, but schedules can go awry when the proper materials do not show up on site, if there is insufficient skilled labor, if there are coordination issues or weather problems, and so forth. Delays can be very expensive, not only in terms of increased cost for extended general conditions and escalation but also in lost revenue when projects open late (especially true for projects that generate monthly cash flow, such as retail, hospitality, office buildings, and dormitories). In a literal sense, time is money.

The responsibility for managing the schedule properly rests with the contractor, who is best equipped by skill and experience to handle the choreography of on-site construction activities. However, it's important to note that the contractor does not have total control. Timely decisions are needed from the owner, comprehensive and coordinated documents are needed from the designer, and cooperation is needed up and down the supply chain. Schedule control is a team sport: Everybody's got some skin in the game, which is why schedule compliance is a shared responsibility. This puts the onus on everyone to do their part, thereby eliminating the blame game.

As to weather-related delays, the trend toward off-site prefabrication reduces risk in two ways: first, by producing various building components in a controlled environment and, second, by reducing the time needed for on-site installation. Using BIM technology to model building components and construction logistics helps tremendously in managing the delivery of materials to the site and removing the waste. Some contractors have adopted just-in-time delivery to minimize the need for on-site storage. In addition, a well-managed safety program always saves time by avoiding delays due to accidents. Except for the vicissitudes of weather, the schedule should be managed with a high degree of confidence.

Quality is another source of risk that concerns owners. Will they get the building they expect, properly constructed? This is a critical question because the long-term cost of ownership actually outweighs the initial capital cost by a substantial margin. Sub-standard construction can result in huge exposure over the long term. If the roof leaks or the MEP system fails down the road, repairs can be costly and disruptive, even if covered by warranties. It can sometimes take years for construction-related problems to show up. While the contractor is best equipped to manage activities on the construction site, the architect is best equipped to oversee quality.

To ensure the desired results, it's important to establish quality standards in advance, making them as objective and as measurable as possible. Benchmarking similar projects is a good place to start. Conducting ongoing quality review is much more effective than "punch-listing" at the end of the job because it's far better, faster, and cheaper to avoid mistakes in the first place than to fix them later. Also, with today's complex projects, commissioning is a must, and this process should start well before the building is turned over to the owner.

Another important aspect of quality control is setting up comprehensive training programs for the staff who will operate the project upon completion. Make sure they are familiar with all the relevant manuals, product data, and maintenance protocols. Make sure they can operate the MEP systems as intended (which represent about 35 percent of the capital cost and nearly 100 percent of the operating cost). Don't forget training programs for the occupants to make sure they understand basic safety procedures.

A building can be well designed and well constructed, but things can still go wrong. Hurricanes, tornadoes, earthquakes, tsunamis, accidents, and labor strikes, while rare, do happen. For these catastrophic events, which are truly unpredictable, insurance is available, and it's relatively cheap because the odds against such occurrences are so great.

Speaking of insurance, current practice is that each entity involved in the project is separately insured.

This makes sense because each one works on a number of simultaneous projects with entirely different circumstances and participants. This insurance is not free, however; it's part of each firm's overhead and is therefore built into the cost of a project. Now imagine that everyone was insured by the same carrier. Should a claim occur, the settlement process would be relatively quick and painless since the insurance company would essentially be negotiating with itself, merely shifting dollars from one pocket to another.

Let's extend that notion slightly. If owners indemnified the project team members from all liability (except for willful negligence), then the cost of individual insurance policies would surely go down dramatically. The savings could then be used to purchase a project-specific policy that would cover the whole team. Such an umbrella policy would serve to eliminate the defensive behavior that drives people apart when problems occur. Instead of asking "Whose fault is it?" the team would be asking "How can we work together to fix this?" A project-based policy would put everyone on the same side of that question.

Changing the Dynamics

With a few simple tweaks, it should be possible to change the basic dynamics of how risk is managed in the A/E/C industry. Owners need to accept the fact that they are the primary decision makers as well as the primary beneficiaries and therefore carry the most responsibility and the most risk. It doesn't help to pretend otherwise. Attempting to shift too much risk to others only complicates the proceedings and has the unintended consequence of increasing the likelihood of suboptimal results. There's really not much mystery to controlling scope, cost, or quality. The schedule can be effectively managed by the use of technology for design, documentation, and site logistics, plus more off-site prefabrication. Project-based insurance policies would eliminate CYA behavior.

The biggest improvements often come from the simplest ideas. Using a single contract that aligns the interests of the owner, architect, and contractor puts everyone on the same side. When everybody has skin in the game, the odds of success go way up because everyone is looking out for each other's interests. This is the fundamental principal of IPD. Design and construction will always carry some inherent risk, of course, but it's much better to embrace and manage risk than to try hiding it or shifting it to others. In other words, the more risk you consciously accept, the safer you will be.

PROFESSIONAL SERVICES: BUILDING THE DREAM

Professional services are at the heart of the design mission. This is where your passion and talent can find their true expression. Don't forget that professional services include integrating the work of your colleagues and consultants. The drawings, models, and specifications you create are merely the tangible products of this most important phase, but remember that they are only instruments of service. The true value of professional services lies in idea generation and problem-solving. Create a culture where people can do their best work and let them surprise you with extraordinary results.

VALUE BY DESIGN

To most people, architecture is a building — a place to go, a place to work, a place to live. In this regard, architecture is viewed as a product: the end result of a creative process. For many years, this product-focused thinking has defined the architecture profession and has been the mother's milk upon which many generations of aspiring designers have been raised. Students are taught to draw and make models in anticipation of creating objects that will eventually become buildings.

In school, the pragmatic aspects of program or budget are often given short shrift: Students work unfettered by practical constraints. This is not altogether a bad thing. Upon entering the real world of professional practice, however, many newly minted graduates must feel like Gulliver — tied down by the constraints of a thousand gossamer threads. Building codes, zoning restrictions, budget limitations, public design review processes, low fees, and "unreasonable" client demands all have a very real impact on the design process.

This should come as no surprise. After all, school is not real life for designers any more than it is for doctors or lawyers. It takes some time to merge the aspirations of the ivory tower with lessons from day-to-day practice. This collision of idealism and pragmatism often leads to a great deal of angst for architects and their clients, but the frustration is wholly unnecessary. Instead, what is needed is a better appreciation of what architects and engineers do. Architects provide so many different kinds of services to so many different constituencies that sometimes they have a hard time communicating the value of what they do. Not surprisingly, clients are equally confused.

What is the real value of design? Design value might seem slippery and elusive, but it needn't be. One simple definition is that value is cost divided by benefit. How much do you pay for something, and what do you get in return? Was it worth the price? Those are the essential questions.

Let's take a simple example, such as a commission for a new office building. Most likely, the client is a developer whose primary interest is in erecting a structure, securing leases, and then reselling the project to an owner with a longer-term financial interest, such as a pension fund. Hence, the primary criterion is that the project must provide a reasonable return on investment; otherwise, it simply won't be built. When the commission is awarded, the specific users are probably unknown because the leases have yet to be signed, but the owner knows that the building must appeal to a broad market. Clearly, controlling capital cost is an issue, as are the interests of various stakeholders such as public review agencies that will have jurisdiction over the project.

How does the architect create value in this situation? The answer includes, but goes way beyond, design aesthetics. Creating value means that the architect can show the owner how to get the most efficient use of the site — maximizing the rentable floor area ratio and the parking and overcoming inherent difficulties such as unusual soil conditions or onerous zoning restrictions.

Design value also means that the appearance of the building will attract potential tenants and in turn their staff and customers. It should be a place that people will want to come to and work in, with a flexible floor plan that will be easily marketed and leased. It may even attract premium rents by virtue of its location or attention-getting design. Value also means that the building materials will be chosen not only for appearance, color, and texture but also for durability. Smart owners know that it costs far more to maintain a building over its useful life than it does to build it in the first place.

Value means providing for flexibility. Since the architect doesn't know who will occupy the building, the design must accommodate a variety of potential users, some of whom will have very different and changing needs over the years. The architect can also provide value by helping secure permits and other necessary public approvals.

Value also means managing the construction cost and schedule efficiently. After all, time is money. If the project can be brought on line at or below prevailing rates for construction cost or delivered earlier than expected, this puts real money in the client's pocket.

Could the architect assist with graphics and signage, creating the marketing image for the building or even, through business contacts, arrange for the client to meet prospective tenants? How about arranging for publicity? All of these aspects reinforce the architect's goal of providing additional value. It should be readily apparent from this simple example that the designer's potential value to a client is as much strategic as aesthetic.

To be truly effective, architects, engineers, and designers must understand and communicate how their services support the client's business mission. When measured this way, the design fee becomes a non-issue because value (cost divided by benefit) always exceeds the cost.

In fact, good design always creates value in excess of cost — otherwise, why do it? A good design decision adds value for many years, and a bad one hurts for just as long. Top-quality design skills should be highly leveraged. Architects who fail to understand this principle risk becoming low-cost providers of a commodity service.

By virtue of your design skill, show your clients how you can create unexpected value in all aspects of your services. This means reconceptualizing professional practice from product-based to process-based and outcome-based. Architects are not just providers of design documentation; they are navigators who help clients achieve their strategic goals. Drawing and specifications are instruments of service, but they are not the essence of the service itself. In other words, don't just draw the lines, help draw the conclusions.

QUESTIONS

1. How well do you understand the client's value drivers?
2. How can you show clients that you can create value in all aspects of the project?
3. What distinguishes your firm from others?

"I see you decided not to go with the glass ceilings?"

HYPERTRACK: SETTING NEW STANDARDS FOR CLIENT SERVICE

The challenging economy has spawned a number of new firms that can compete for work without high overhead. Technology has made the production of sophisticated drawings faster and cheaper. Even high-profile commissions often include some measure of price competition. Talented staff is harder to find and more expensive to recruit. Each of these factors puts a lot of pressure on fees and profitability. When the market is hot, so is the competition, and when the market is slow, sharpening your business skills is essential to survival.

Smart firms don't wait for the economy to improve or for owners to offer higher fees. Instead, they are busy thinking up new ways to provide service that will enable them to remain profitable even as fees are going down. While this may seem counterintuitive, the truth is that it is not only possible, it is necessary. After all, clients themselves are facing similar pressures — they are constantly under the gun to produce higher quality products and services faster and cheaper, and they expect their design consultants not only to keep pace but to lead the way with new ideas about how to do it. Understanding how competitive pressures affect your client's business as well as your own is a key to becoming a leader in the new economy.

"The task of a leader is to show staff the benefits of change."

STEVE FISKUM

To stay competitive and therefore valuable, throw out all of your old assumptions about how you "should" do business. Think unexpected, contrary, and outrageous thoughts. Align your organization with your client's interests first, forming a new kind of virtual partnership that can accomplish amazing things by breaking down traditional client/architect barriers. Prepare to be surprised by the creativity and productivity from every member of your team, no matter what their role or responsibility.

Here's an example. A design firm was engaged by a large biotechnology company that owned a parcel of land. The company was unsure about how to put this property to best use: Should it be sold for a profit, developed, leased, or land-banked? In the course of the analysis, the architect became aware of a local down-zoning petition that threatened to reduce allowable floor-area ratio by nearly 40 percent, greatly affecting the asset value of the land.

This was an important wakeup call. The client needed to decide very quickly about the best use of the property or risk losing more than $30 million in asset value. Naturally, this got the immediate attention of senior management.

Even though the owner did not know what kind of project, if any, made sense on the site or whether or not the company would ultimately occupy a new building for their own purposes, it was clear that being passive was the worst possible strategy. A special project team was formed that could quickly explore a variety of alternatives and take action.

The team included geotechnical engineers, MEP engineers, structural engineers, legal counsel, and construction management and real estate advisors. The client chose the architect to manage all the consultants. Communications were immediately set up with key personnel at city hall, and since the client's business was based in another state, great care was taken to ensure that strict protocols were followed in the submission of all materials for review and approval by city agencies.

One of the most pressing goals was submitting a permit set of construction drawings and specifications as soon as possible for a building that had no program, no budget, and no design. When the client gave formal approval to proceed for this filing, the deadline was less than 30 days away. In just three and a half weeks, a comprehensive set of shell-and-core documents for a speculative 360,000-square-foot project was completed and submitted to the city for detailed review. The project was designed completely "by right" and was carefully fit on an unusual trapezoidal site that had almost no street frontage.

The schedule and the design challenge both seemed impossible at first, and this required a new way of organizing the effort. Weekly coordination meetings were held, special task groups were set up to explore specific issues in detail, and each member of the team was given a clear role and responsibility. Decisions were delegated freely, made quickly, and confirmed at daily coordination meetings.

Even though the effort was intense, there was no panic or need for excessive overtime. In fact, the architects and engineers finished the drawings a day early. This unusual process, which was dubbed "HyperTrack," worked for a number of reasons:

1. **The client committed a full-time project leader who was available to make decisions on the spot as needed.** In addition, the owner committed a number of his own in-house experts to process information quickly and provide instant feedback.

2. **The design firm provided office space on its own premises for the client's team leader, installed special phone lines, and assigned dedicated administrative staff to the project.** The firm also provided a clearinghouse for all information and scheduling, issuing meeting notes within 24 hours so that everyone was continually up-to-date.

3. **To get things done quickly, it was important to provide "frictionless paperwork."** Communication was done via

email, and drawings were posted on a project website for easy access, downloading, and transmittal of revisions. Documents were instantly accessible from any location, including the owner's out-of-state headquarters.

4. **Business arrangements were kept simple.** All consultants were paid on an hourly basis with a built-in profit margin and a guaranteed 30-day turnaround on invoices. This enabled the team to focus on the job at hand rather than how to get paid or how to manage time to meet a budget. Ultimately, the cost of the construction documents was about 20 percent less than traditional benchmarks would have predicted, so the client received excellent value for the money.

5. **A lot of attention was paid to getting the right team on the job.** Consultants were selected not only for their professional expertise but for their cooperative attitude and the ability to commit high-level decision makers whenever needed. Team morale was kept high by providing lunches and snacks for in-house meetings. There were also occasional dinners out and outings to baseball games and harbor cruises. This helped develop personal trust at all levels of the team.

Throughout this process, the design team was able to see things through the eyes of the client. They knew which issues were critical and how they could contribute their expertise to create meaningful solutions. Each task was approached from a perspective of *How are we going to work together to get this done?* rather than *How did we do this the last time?* Team members at all levels were made to feel important because they were important. In fact, some of the most creative and productive ideas came from less-experienced technical staff. And while the project required a lot of hard work, it was also fun.

The upshot was that the owner was able to proceed with the project in record time and at much lower cost than originally anticipated. Speed proved to be an enormous strategic advantage because each month of schedule acceleration was worth $1 million in revenue flow to the project when completed. The process proved to be so successful that certain aspects of it are being studied for adoption as corporate-wide policy. None of this would have been possible if the owner and the design team had been intimidated by the constraints of past practice. What does this example mean for your firm and how you do business?

- Know your clients exceedingly well — their goals, their resources and their pressures. What are they really trying to accomplish and why?
- Keep your focus on results, and do only what has to be done. Avoid the temptation to be sidetracked.
- Use your team resources to devise a new kind of process: Figure out where the barriers in the system are and then remove them.
- Understand that time is money, and know when to spend lots of it in order to generate even greater savings.
- Focus on flexibility. Make the decisions that you need to make in order to move the project forward, but be ready to change at a moment's notice.

By aligning your culture with that of your client, you can redesign the design process. In doing so, even in a competitive market, you will have no clear differentiation.

Questions

1. How will you align your work process with your client's culture?
2. How can you make speed an asset rather than a liability?
3. What are you doing now that should be done differently or not at all?

How Technology is Redesigning Design

True innovation crushes standards. When new tools and techniques are applied to a time-honored process, everything changes. The industrial revolution dramatically altered means and methods. The advent of automobiles irrevocably changed our ideas about time and distance. With the invention of television, the world shrank to the size of a global village. Sometimes change is obvious and sometimes it is subtle, but it always has a long-lasting effect.

In just a few years, there has been a profound and permanent change brought about by sophisticated design technology. This has affected not only the way we produce design documents but also the very way we think about design. Technology has forever changed both process and product. Those who have embraced technology enthusiastically and understand its implications are reinventing their practices. They are marketing differently, designing differently, managing differently, and becoming more profitable in the process.

> ***"A variety of technologies will disrupt many of today's firms and create tomorrow's great organizations."***
> CLAYTON CHRISTENSEN

With the advent of e-commerce, limitless possibilities are emerging. Just like the changes brought about by steam engines, cars and television, the Internet has recast all of our fundamental assumptions about time, space, and communication. There are five aspects of this seismic shift in both process and product that are reshaping how design is done:

1. **Image quality.** In the past, architectural drawings were relatively abstract, collapsing three-dimensional information into two dimensions. Plans, sections, and elevations were the common language used to illustrate design ideas. It's now possible to render highly realistic images in three dimensions, including color, shadow, texture, and even animation and sound. The "drawings" themselves have morphed into "cyberplaces" defined by bits and bytes. Nothing is "real" about computer-generated imagery, yet these images are much more realistic than anything drawn by hand.

2. **Speed.** Design technology allows faster drafting and rendering, speedier revisions, and quicker printing. This is a tremendous advantage because it enables designers to consider many more alternatives at less cost, thus improving overall quality.

3. **Accuracy.** For area calculations, materials takeoff, engineering calculations, dimensional coordination, and the like, accuracy standards have forever been altered by design technology. Precision is now a presumption.

4. **Complex visualization.** When it was unveiled in 1962, Eero Saarinen's TWA Terminal in New York was audacious and breathtaking. With today's technology, the building's compound curves could be generated, engineered, and tested with relative ease. Since the software for this complex visualization originated in the aerospace and entertainment industries, we also see a blurring of professional boundaries. Is the future of design rooted in art, entertainment, or technology? The answer, of course, is all three.

5. **Quality.** Technology provides an entirely new way of making architecture. Clients, no longer alienated and confused

> by old-fashioned abstract working drawings, are able to be much more active participants in the process. Technology allows architects to communicate with clients and the public much more clearly and convincingly than ever before, and there is a direct and palpable effect on overall quality.

Architects and engineers may still believe they are in the business of designing buildings, but with technology they are doing it in very different ways. In a sense, the process of design has been "microwaved." When you make popcorn, do you get out the pan, heat the oil, pop the corn, melt the butter, and then clean up? Or do you toss a specially prepared packet into the microwave, set the timer for three minutes, and enjoy an equally tasty snack faster, better, and cheaper?

In a similar way, technology has restored the essence of the design process. In the future, architects will have entirely new ways of creating and communicating design ideas to their clients, contractors, and the public. Smart design firms are pushing this technology to its limits. They are redesigning what design can do.

In fact, computers may enable us to invent a whole new language of "spatial notation," much like sheet music. With only a few abstract symbols, it is possible to "write" music on paper (a two-dimensional medium) that captures and communicates ideas of melody and rhythm. Musical notation is simple, comprehensive, and elegant — and it can be understood universally by musicians playing any instrument anywhere in the world. Complex symphonies or operas, requiring dozens of players with different kinds of instruments ("tools"), are all based on the same straightforward language of musical notation, easily learned in grade school, that can provides an astonishing degree of artistic freedom.

Why haven't designers developed such a language? It should be possible to describe space, color, texture, and construction details with equal poetry and clarity. With such a language, the way we go about doing design will be faster, cheaper, better, and more imaginative. The demands of our clients and the public will make it necessary. The power of technology will make it possible.

QUESTIONS

1. How is technology changing your practice?
2. How does technology change how you communicate with clients?
3. What resource and staffing changes will you make to stay technically current?

"How were we ever pofitable before the BIM-integrated iPhone?

ROI: "Return on Innovation"

One lesson to be learned from studying successful firms is that they are making a sharp break with old habits, deliberately adopting new modes of behavior. A design organization is a complex socio-technical system whose ability to thrive depends on the proper blend of talent, skill, and strategy. Over time, there has been a steadily increasing demand on design organizations that will become even more pronounced in the coming years. With change comes choice. It takes both courage and intellectual honesty — not only talent — to look at the world anew.

Here are several trends already underway that are likely to accelerate within the next few years. Think about these issues as they relate to your own organization.

1. **Digital innovation will provide new communication solutions.** Capacity, processing speed, and portability will increase exponentially. The implications on communications, productivity, and client relations are profound.

2. **Design-build will occur in the majority of projects.** There is no doubt now that this is becoming a preferred delivery option for clients seeking a single point of responsibility and accountability.

3. **Changes in zoning laws will encourage mixed-use projects and clustered communities.** Expect to see stores, schools, cafes, and service centers co-located with residences. This change is driven by driven by security, environment, and transportation concerns among people in pursuit of a better sense of community.

4. **The use of nanotechnology will explode.** Expect so see nanotech leveraged in sophisticated robots on construction sites, in office tools, and even in clothing that contains built-in computers and heating elements that could make thin jackets the preferred option for construction workers, skiers, and travelers.

5. **Health care professionals, management consultants, and technology professionals will overlap with the design professions.** These specialist content providers will become the fastest-growing professions in the next few years. Some management consultants will expand services and further blur traditional service delivery boundaries, taking more market share.

6. **Recognition will be given to "knowledge entrepreneurs" as the solution providers of the future.** Those who hold production jobs will increasingly move to the lower levels of the food chain and become less influential. Expect increased outsourcing of labor, even for specialized professionals.

7. **China will not only be the largest population but also the world's largest economy.** China will become the world's largest design marketplace. The country will increasingly export design talent and services and become a global competitor in production.

8. **Architectural offices will be driven by big data.** Design firms can be repositories for facility management documentation, restoration, renovation, and maintenance. Highly advanced data centers will become critical hubs for architecture, engineering, and interior design decisions.

9. **Large organizations will be increasingly vulnerable to Internet-only companies and smaller, more nimble solution providers.** Fifty percent of all goods and services

will be sold electronically, with no huge physical infrastructure requirements.

10. **Renewable energy sources like wind, solar, and fuel cells will finally become cost efficient.** Advances are taking place in "green tech" businesses that will make wind energy a viable choice for a variety of residential and commercial building types. Cornfields can easily become wind fields.

11. **Illumination balloons/portable suns will aid in nighttime construction projects.** This will allow for quicker turnaround and more control and will be applicable for road construction, building projects, and commercial applications.

12. **Cities will operate 24/7.** There is an efficiency factor and a value proposition for cities that follow the Las Vegas, New York City, Miami, and London models, resulting in better use of time, energy, and resources.

13. **There will be mega-growth in hotels and resorts.** Expect larger cruises, which are essentially mobile man-made islands. Planning for space station resorts is now underway, and there will be permanent entertainment centers in space within the next 50 years. Hospitality and entertainment design will be in high demand.

14. **Green and sustainable design will become mainstream.** Hydrogen fuel cell technology will be a safe and economical option. "Green design" will advance well beyond 20th-century initiatives. Electric cars or electric-combustion hybrids will be the norm. The majority of waste will be recycled into resources.

15. **Security will become a key consideration in urban design, product design, process design, and building**

design. Understanding the relationship between security and design, and the designer's role in that relationship will be paramount. Methods for detection and deterrence will evolve as threats that drive the need for security planning become more sophisticated

16. **All financial transactions will be electronic.** All taxes will be filed electronically, all invoices will be emailed, and smart cards will substitute for cash. Accountability and security will be much improved.

17. **Material composites will replace traditional metals in buildings.** Ceramic buildings will gain popularity as sand is cheap and easily recycled. Recycled materials will be the majority of the structure in new bridges, docks, and buildings. Plastics also have great potential.

18. **Commercial and institutional environments will increasingly become part of the "edutainment" or "experience" economy.** Shopping centers, children's hospitals, schools, and offices will become spaces that make people feel good and elevate the human spirit.

19. **Personal computers and phones will include interactive screens.** Each device will include a camera and will enable better communication in and out of the office. Computerized self-care in medicine will become commonplace, including diagnostics and real-time dialogue with health care providers.

20. **The skills of innovation and optimism will be the most highly sought after by corporations.** Strategic problem solving will be a prime skill set in the emerging economy. Intelligence combined with optimism will be highly attractive to employers and clients alike.

You should always be ready for surprises, disruptions, and accidental events. The most successful firms will stay nimble and resilient because they will have a culture of idea generation.

QUESTIONS

1. What future changes could disrupt your firm?
2. How will you be resilient in the face of change?
3. Assume that you cannot fail. How will this affect your planning?

"Are you from the future?"

Redefining Design Teams

We have experienced some practical new insights about a mysterious subject — the decision-thinking processes of the human mind as it relates to design teams. Design requires judgment. When designers choose among different alternatives, it is rarely between right and wrong. Small differences among equally viable options can make a big difference in the ultimate outcome. Even when decisions are relatively small, they can have big consequences.

Historically, design organizations have operated as professional silos. They separate functions, looking for precision and focus, and as a consequence, they often separate processes. Job descriptions are too often written in ways that narrow, rather than expand, a person's role.

These well-intended job descriptions anchor people and the teams they affect. They are often not good for much except to reinforce and recognize organizational boundaries, and they almost always miss the big picture. "That's not my job," is a common refrain, but what is not understood is that this frame of mind is self-centered and ultimately leads to a hardening of the organization's arteries.

> ***"Differences can be creative. ... Find ways to allow people to express their innate talents rather than prove their compliance to a firm or cultural norm."***
>
> DESIGN INTELLIGENCE

Leading design firms are learning how to blur the boundaries. Some are hiring product experts from the manufacturers right into the firm as active project participants. A health care design firm has brought in a retired doctor and hospital administrator. An industrial design firm has brought in an industrial psychologist. All are key members of the design team.

Great team effort requires expanding the definition of what it means to be a designer. Think big, learn to be inclusive, and reap the rewards.

QUESTIONS

1. How do you organize design teams in your firm?
2. What changes are needed in order to enhance collaboration?
3. How will integrating other professionals strengthen your own design team?
4. How will you integrate all the design disciplines to better service clients?

Keeping Priorities on Track

One of the biggest problems with maintaining project profitability is keeping each phase of work on schedule and within budget. There is a great temptation to design until you "get it right," even if this means using up fees earmarked for subsequent phases.

Continual design refinements made during the construction documentation (CD) and construction administration (CA) phases are common and usually take more time than anticipated. Subsequent pressure get bid packages out as soon as possible often results in incomplete or poorly coordinated documents. This only puts additional pressure on construction administration — a traditional money-loser for most firms. Throughout the process, designers and managers are often at odds — each one wants to drive the bus and neither wants to be a passenger.

The key to solving this problem is understanding that regardless of where they sit, everybody is riding on the same bus. Design is a process that starts with marketing and does not end until the ribbon is cut when the building opens. A successful project requires more skills than any single individual can possibly provide alone, including marketing, management, design, and technology, as well as financial and political skills.

If your office is divided into separate tribes of designers, managers, and technicians, each of whom owns a piece of the process sequentially, then you have unwittingly created a culture that will always be at odds with itself. While each aspect of the process is critical, it is the blend and balance among them that determines ultimate success.

The key to getting it right is to create mutually dependent stakeholders. Designers are beholden to marketers because designers have nothing to do until a project is landed. They are equally beholden to the technicians and the construction administrators who see to it that their design ideas can be properly carried out. Likewise, technicians and construction administrators depend on design vision to guide their work. No one can function without the accounting staff, who send the bills, collect the money, and write the checks.

If people commandeer more than their share of resources — time, money or staff — an imbalance occurs, and it is an absolute certainty that the project will suffer in some important way. There are two essential aspects to getting it right. The first is to communicate clearly about what you expect of others on the team. The second is to understand what they expect of you.

You cannot have a successful project unless all team members deliver the goods together in concert. This means that if you don't hold up your end of the bargain, everyone else pays the price. For example, if a designer persists in making changes long after design development has been approved by the client, it is very likely that there will be problems with the construction documents, shop drawings, or changes in the field. Ultimately, the only way to make sure that a project will be properly executed is to provide enough time during construction administration to get it right.

What about the notion that you can just take cost overruns out of the profit? After all, isn't it better to spend a little more to get great design even if profitability suffers? While at first glance this is a beguiling notion, it is a siren song. Running a loss on a project is an extremely expensive tax on your future. Smart organizations understand that healthy profits are the only way to ensure long-term success of the firm. There can be no room in the corporate culture for design vs. management conflict; they must be aligned. Instead, promote the firm-wide value that design and management are not only mutually dependent, but they are mutually necessary. Design is a process of employing resources (time, talent, money) to create a purposeful and desirable result. So is management.

This balancing of design and management requires a great deal of discipline. Great design starts in the marketing phase and blossoms as the team juggles the constraints of program, budget, site, and schedule with practical and aesthetic issues. It continues when these fertile ideas are condensed and then frozen into the single option, chosen from among the many, that will actually get built. Design matures during the construction phase, when ideas on paper find life in real built space. By viewing all of these phases as part of a single design continuum, you can provide your staff with a framework with which to understand their respective roles and responsibilities.

It's ironic that great buildings, like great art, have more to do with knowing when to stop than how to start. What would have happened to the *Pieta* if Michelangelo had spent another year on it? What happens to a cake if you don't take it out of the oven on time? In school, budding young designers are encouraged to explore as many options and alternatives as possible. But in professional practice, the best design comes from the wisdom of knowing how to choose the best option and then making it work.

Once this choice is made, it must be executed with a great deal of commitment and confidence. This requires both the discipline and the generosity to make sure that all phases of the work have the resources of time and talent required for success. Robbing Peter to pay Paul simply doesn't work.

QUESTIONS

1. What process habit patterns are slowing down services and compromising client satisfaction?

2. Is your firm design-driven or management-driven?

3. How will you reinforce the proper balance?

4. How will your firm design both faster and better?

Blurring Boundaries

Do you think of yourself as a design manager? An interior designer? A design engineer? Do your employees think of themselves in traditional ways that relate solely to their education or their state registration certificate? According to our research with the thought leaders in the industry, if designers don't redefine their job descriptions and expand their view of the profession, they may destroy the very thing they are trying to protect. Progress comes not from perfecting yourself within the confines of a defined role; it comes from the courage to experiment and change.

There is a blurring of boundaries in design that will no doubt accelerate in the future. This is also true among other professions, such as medicine, and law.

A client approached an architectural firm to help solve a complex strategic problem. A design problem, yes, but it was also about branding, global facility design, and the development of a better business model. The firm, a diversified architectural firm, had not been asked to provide this specific service in the past. However, its track record with this client was strong and its stock was high. The client needed innovative problem-solvers and didn't care to turn elsewhere for solutions. This category of service wasn't mentioned in the firm's marketing literature, but in the client's eyes, the firm was staffed with outstanding innovators.

This client had a service gap to fill. The architect and his staff went to work imagining how they might fill that gap to provide the best solutions for the client. They looked again at what they thought their firm was all about. Their openness to re-evaluating their own abilities not only led to a breakthrough solution for the client but also resulted in the development of a new core competency. The firm is now positioned for more strategic consulting at the highest policy level.

> ***"An idea can turn to dust or magic, depending on the talent that rubs against it."***
> BILL BERNBACH

In another example, an architect was leading a design team for a new conference center for the disabled. When it was discovered that there was no computer workstation on the market that would allow the disabled user to operate it without assistance, the architect designed and oversaw the manufacture of a prototype with a variety of movable components. The delighted client authorized mass production of a previously nonexistent product. In today's practice, these are just a couple of examples of the many unique forms of value capture that design firms have discovered.

Innovation happens in many ways, by ingenuity and openness to unexpected opportunity, by jumping outside the comfort zone and into the zone of experimentation. It often leads to new value and to revolutionary new success models.

In the future, there will be even more blurring of those traditional boundaries, resulting in greater opportunities and enhanced satisfaction. All that is required is the desire and ability to work with, rather than against, the forces of change.

QUESTIONS

1. How will you redefine job descriptions in your firm?

2. How will you and your firm be more innovative?

3. What is your work for?

Design Makes the Difference

Good design is not just a thing: the final building or product. It is also a central part of the business process and how your firm is organized and managed, how employees are hired and trained, and how the marketing process creates new projects and client relationships. The design of your organization — its processes and output — is what we call enterprise design.

> ***"The ultimate creation is the process of creativity itself."***
> DESIGN FUTURES COUNCIL

The Design/Enterprise model is a crucial element of success. You want to do great work, make a reasonable profit, and have fun in ways that are meaningful to you and to your clients. Don't lose sight of these goals. To help you navigate the future, consider these principles that have been collected from the leaders of the most successful design firms in the world:

- Get on with the reinvention of your own sustainable future and be an entrepreneur of your life.
- Expect business down-cycles. See them as an opportunity. Look for new possibilities in a world of constant change — an economy where design will be even more important. By maintaining financial control, you maintain creative control.
- Design your life and your firm's future not just around meeting your client's current tangible needs but by going beyond the ordinary to strengthen your enterprise.

- Organize each day around your priorities. Act with purpose and make each day count.
- Build a community of trust in all of your relationships.
- Laugh — it's a barometer of a healthy attitude.
- Be known for your resilience and your ability to achieve results, even during times of uncertainty.
- Be an authority, but also be a role model of balance, judgment, and constant learning.

Creating satisfaction is one of the key values for all in the design professions. Remember that it's the people and not the organization that really matters. Managing change is a core competency for leadership. In the future, design will be more important than ever before. Through design, better communities are created, the economy improves, and the quality of life is enhanced. As a designer, you are in a unique position of influence with your clients, colleagues, and community. Embrace change while you can. Leverage your design skills to make a difference — the value chain will not be complete without you.

Questions

1. What are your top three goals as a design professional?
2. What does good design mean to you? How does this differ from mainstream conventions?
3. How do you measure design value?

FINANCES
Getting Your Reward

Doing work without getting paid is not a winning strategy. Leaders must realize that to create a vibrant and productive design enterprise, good financial management is just as important as design skill. Money is the fuel that enables you to practice design to the best of your ability, and profits are needed to finance growth — including new equipment, talented staff, and appropriate workspace. For many architects and engineers, finance is too often a foreign language, but this need not be the case. By understanding a few simple principles and applying them consistently, you'll be able to spend more productive time doing better design, and you'll eliminate worry about paying the rent. Remember that your clients are already fluent in the language of finance, so if you want to enhance their success, and yours as well, it pays to understand that money is a design tool.

THE PHILOSOPHY OF PROFIT

In the design profession, complaints about compensation are common. Architects often compare their earning power unfavorably with doctors, lawyers, and sometimes even plumbers. They resent that clients don't seem to recognize the value of what they do, or pay "fair" fees. Yet research shows that the client community has considerable respect for architects and values their professional advice. So why is it so hard for most firms to generate a decent bottom line?

> ***"Fear of new ideas makes us less valuable."***
> DAVE ZIMMERMAN

There are several reasons. By far the most important is the attitude about profitability that pervades the profession, plus the fundamental misunderstanding about what profitability really means. Design is a curious blend of the creative and the technical. It is not always clear at the start of a project what the final result will be — that's part of the discovery and delight of design. Since the required level of effort is somewhat indeterminate and can change significantly over the life of a project, fees based on a presumed cost structure for producing the work are almost always guaranteed to be wrong. As the project evolves, additional unanticipated effort, if uncompensated, inevitably erodes the bottom line.

Too many design professionals believe that profit is what's left over at the end of a job. This is a sure recipe for failure. Instead, think of profit as a cost of doing business, just like rent, salaries, or any other overhead item. Build it into your project planning and your design process. Profit is an essential part of running a design firm; it is necessary for investing in growth, new staff, new technology, and better workspace. A firm that is not making a healthy profit is robbing itself of the ability to produce work to the best of its ability. Viewed this way, profit is actually one of your most important design tools. A chronic lack of profit is like a disease that attacks a firm's vital organs. You can't afford this and neither can your clients.

Would you willingly patronize a doctor or a lawyer who had trouble paying bills and was on the verge of bankruptcy? No, and neither would your clients. Since many clients are business minded, they appreciate good business sense in others and understand that the fees they pay must cover the basic cost of doing business and a reasonable return on investment. At the same time, clients are seeking value — they want real benefit for the fees they are paying. Very often what happens is that the architect is tempted to perform services that are not needed or required by the client because the architect desires these elements. This only adds cost — not value — to the project.

REGENERATIVE FINANCIAL MODEL

	Decline				Sustainable				Regenerative			
FUTURE SCAN												
PROFIT %	-5	-3	-2	0	3	5	8	10	13	17	20	25
CHARACTERISTICS	Failing		Below Ave.			Ave.		Above Ave.			Best of Class	

What Is a Fair Return?

For firms that are willing to concentrate on adding measurable value for their clients, profits in the range of 10 percent to 15 percent and even higher are quite feasible. Remember that the higher your legitimate profit, the better able you will be to serve clients.

There are several ways to achieve better profitability. Ironically, the most important aspect of profitability has nothing to do with money; it has to do with thoroughly understanding your clients' needs, constraints, resources, and decision-making style. At the onset of a new project or client relationship, ask:

- What does the client hope to achieve?
- What does the client value? How will it be measured?
- How can you help create that value?

When the answers to these questions are understood, you will have established the basis for an effective fee negotiation — one that benefits both sides. Don't concentrate on how much you are likely to make. That only clouds the issue from the client's perspective and your own. Instead, concentrate on how your firm is uniquely qualified to help your clients realize their goals. Be specific. With this in mind, a reasonable fee — one that includes the opportunity for profit — is much easier to establish.

Good Design Creates Good Value

What about clients that have set predetermined fee limits or that select design services primarily on the basis of low cost? When the fee limits are set before negotiation begins, as is often the case in public work, negotiate on the basis of scope or schedule rather than cost. Provide what is reasonable for the fee available, and don't over-promise results.

Make sure you agree on what circumstances trigger additional services, and then be vigilant about requesting the fees when circumstances warrant. Pressure on fees can actually be helpful because it forces firms to critically assess their production processes and weed out policies, procedures, and even staff that are not cost effective. Under economic pressure, many companies have experienced the sweeping changes of re-engineering, which is a fundamental reconfiguration of how a business is organized and how it produces goods and services. Design firms are not and should not be immune from this process.

In fact, you should welcome a serious discussion about value with any client, and then show how you are going to deliver the goods. Good design always creates good value. Be prepared to demonstrate how, and your negotiations will be much more productive.

Know What Kind of Work to Pursue

One of the most important ways to achieve profitability is through strategic marketing: knowing what kind of work to pursue and, equally important, what not to pursue. If you understand the talent in your firm and how to make best use of it, you will be more focused in your marketing and better able to secure jobs for which you are truly qualified and therefore highly competitive.

Don't waste time chasing projects with a low probability of success or those with high risk and low return. And when you land a good one, negotiate intelligently to ensure there is a win/win outcome for all concerned. If you take on risk, insist on appropriate compensation. For example, when hiring consultants, don't forget to charge a premium to account for the management, communication, coordination, billing, and liability associated with their work; these are legitimate costs of doing business and you should be paid fairly to provide the services. Don't accept uncompensated risk — it's a mistake for all concerned and sure to be a drain on profits.

Communicate Project Goals

When the job is landed and the contract terms are set, make sure that the entire design team understands the financial parameters of the job. People perform best when they are informed; they have to know what's important and how their activities make a difference not only to the design but also to the bottom line.

This is not to say that you should be running your design firm like a bank or an insurance company, with money as the sole focus, but it does mean that good design and good management are complementary — one is not possible without the other. Bear in mind that project losses are extremely expensive. For example, if a project loses $100,000, it would take an entirely new $10 million job at a 10 percent fee and a 10 percent profit as well as several years of effort just to get back that lost revenue. Losses on individual projects are not isolated, short-term events: Their effect is felt far into the future. Project losses are like a heavy tax on your organization.

The philosophy of profitability is fundamental. Without profits, your ability to deliver top-quality design service is compromised, and the future of your firm is in jeopardy. While you may not be able to guarantee a profit on every single job, you can greatly increase your probability with a few simple steps: Understand your clients' goals, demonstrate your value, negotiate effectively, and manage with vigilance.

Finally, remember that profit is not a dirty word. Profitability is good for your firm and it is also good for your clients. A firm that is financially healthy is in a position to do a much better job than one that is suffering. And doing good work the ultimate bottom line.

Questions

1. Why are clients attracted to design firms that are well managed?
2. What level of profit do you need to practice successfully?
3. How will you demonstrate to your clients that good design is good value?

Profitability by Design

For many designers, the financial aspects of the profession are viewed as a necessary evil, something that gets in the way of producing quality design. It is precisely because of this attitude that some design firms find themselves in chronic financial difficulty, unable to pay competitive salaries and bonuses, provide staff training, or acquire the most advanced technology to improve their productivity.

Surprisingly, this phenomenon is not so much related to skill as it is to attitude. It is time that designers, like their best clients, understand that profitability is an essential ingredient in a healthy practice and that good business management skills are not "anti-design" but in fact are the very foundation that supports the firm's design mission.

Some designers still assume that profit is what's left over at the end of a job. Nothing could be further from the truth. Profitability, like good engineering, should be designed into a project at the start, and it begins with the basic assumption that design is a value-adding enterprise.

"Trust is the foundation of leadership."
MIKE ESTEP

Clients want top-quality design. They appreciate and are prepared to pay for professional services that will enable them to meet their goals. Like the rest of us, clients are subject to the market dynamics, and they are acutely aware of the cost/benefit ratio of their decisions. All of this should inform the design process and enable the architect to produce better results.

Understanding Risks and Rewards

Designers are often guilty of "creative interpretation" or willful misunderstanding of the client's specific goals and constraints for the project. When the task at hand is thoroughly understood by both design firm and client, then achieving those goals is greatly simplified.

Next time you are involved in a fee negotiation with a client, ask yourself the following:

- What does the client really need?
- What does the client value?
- How will the client measure the success of the project?
- How does the client quantify cost, value, and price?
- Is the architect selling what the client is buying?

For the negotiated fee to be successful, there needs to be an exchange of value. The client must feel both understood and well served. This leads directly to setting fees that make sense for both sides — fees that include the opportunity for profit.

Profits Regenerate the Future

When negotiating with a client, remember that asking is the first rule of receiving. There must be enough fee on the table to produce the quality results that the client seeks. If both sides understand this, it will be a straightforward transaction. If the fee is not sufficient to provide at least the opportunity for profit, then there is often a fundamental misunderstanding of the scope of the engagement by either the client or the architect. Profits are important because they are necessary to support the design mission of the firm. Breaking even is not good enough. In fact, it's a ticket to oblivion.

Make Growth an Objective

Any creative enterprise needs to grow in order to thrive. This growth can be measured in terms of revenue, staff size, or market penetration. Growth requires fuel — for hiring and training people, acquiring new technology, and business development. Growth is risky, often uncertain, and yet it is growth that keeps an enterprise strong.

Organizations that support growth on a personal and professional level are more likely to attract interesting commissions and talented people. As a result, these firms are better able to produce quality results than those that remain stagnant and hobbled by low profitability. In other words, profit should be seen as a cost of doing business, just like rent or salaries. Managing for profitability will enable a design firm to produce higher quality work, a greater level of client and staff satisfaction, and a much more interesting future.

Market Strategically

The first step toward profitability is to market strategically. Pursue only those commissions for which you know you can add significant value. Many firms waste precious marketing resources (time, money, and talent) chasing jobs for which they are only marginally qualified, resulting in frustration and an abysmal hit rate. By understanding the needs and desires of your prospective clients, you can focus your efforts on those prospects for which you can be realistically competitive. Being a true expert will not only improve your marketing results, but it will give you a leg up in the negotiating process as well.

Negotiate Wisely

Intelligent negotiation is also a crucial step, and good listening is the most important part of negotiation. This requires both a thorough understanding of the commission and a thorough understanding of your cost structure. If the two are not in alignment, you are in trouble before you start. No amount of talent can rescue a bad contract.

Do not negotiate on the price of a job but on the value that will be delivered. This simple principle is often misunderstood. If you are not experienced in negotiation techniques, get help. Recognize that a bad contract hurts both parties. Also recognize that in addition to negotiating a fee, you can negotiate scope, time, deliverables, terms, and level of quality. If there is not a legitimate opportunity for profit in the contract, then you have voluntarily created misfortune before the job even starts. The cost of an unprofitable project is enormous, not just in financial terms but in lost opportunity and staff morale as well. It is like borrowing from the future.

Establish a Simple Tracking System

Once you have negotiated the scope, schedule, and fee, it is extremely important to set up a simple but accurate tracking system that will enable you and your staff to understand the project's status at any time. These tracking systems must be objective and measurable: Do not rely on subjective judgments such as estimates of percent complete.

Many jobs run into trouble because there are no predetermined portions of the fee reserved for specific phases of the project. Hence the last phase, usually construction administration, is guaranteed to run a loss because the team has already run out of fuel. When this happens it is too late to recover. This often leads to quality problems in the field, dissatisfied clients, and frustration all around. Apportioning the fee properly requires discipline and an understanding that all phases of the process are critically important to success. None can be compromised.

Non-Linear Solutions

The design process is iterative, not linear; it circles back on itself. The answers are not clear at the beginning of a job — they have to be discovered during the course of design. Changes in scope, schedule, and cost are not unusual. When this happens, it is time to revisit the terms of the contract and raise the issue of additional services.

Many architects perform additional services as a gesture of goodwill without recognizing the true cost, which can include substantial long-term liability. The recognition of risk and its associated rewards are always part of the profitability equation.

Designers are unique in their potential to deliver value to their clients. This value lasts far beyond the transaction for design services, often extending years into the future. Planning for profit is no different in concept from planning for space or engineering requirements — it needs to be designed into the job at the outset as a clear expectation. Profit is not an accident; it is an essential ingredient of a high-quality professional practice. It is part of what enables you to do your best for clients.

Questions

1. How much profit do you need to stay healthy?

2. When negotiating, are you a good listener? How do you know?

3. How can you avoid performing uncompensated additional services?

Bringing Value to Clients

Professional practice is undergoing unprecedented change. You can be more relevant than ever if you are creative and strategic. There are many new opportunities that will take you far beyond traditional boundaries. Some firms are winning big, profitable new commissions and providing innovative new services, such as energy modeling or facilities management. These firms are finding satisfying challenges, good margins, and a high rate of repeat business. Designers can advocate for innovation beyond traditional problem solving. Architects don't just draft and draw; engineers don't just calculate for structural strength or CFM; landscape architects don't just select plant materials; and interior designers don't just decorate. Unfortunately, these attitudes are still present in many firms. And such stereotypes undercut the level of respect and the perceived value of professional services. Good design can add value for your clients in many ways:

- Good design enhances communication.
- Good design improves safety.
- Good design saves time and money.
- Good design improves staff productivity.
- Good design simplifies use and manufacturing.
- Good design enhances competitiveness and business success.
- Good design improves health and well-being.
- Good design creates beauty and delight.

Successful firms stand apart from the pack. They are leaders — not followers — of creative design. Sometimes they break the rules. Clients notice and they spread the word. They understand that a value driver is neither a firm's brochure nor a catch phrase. Instead, it is a differentiating insight and an ability to put new ideas into action.

QUESTIONS

1. What would you call yourself if you couldn't use your current professional title?
2. How creative is your culture? How do you know?
3. List the ways that you produce value for your clients.

DEMYSTIFYING DESIGN FEES

Designers often complain about low fees and how difficult it is to be profitable when clients expect more service for less money. One of the obvious reasons for this is that clients are reluctant to spend when they don't understand what they are paying for.

Quality design embraces more than aesthetics — it also has a financial dimension. Does this mean that quality design is unimportant to clients or that they don't care what a project looks like? No, they care a great deal, of course, which is why they hire architects and designers in the first place. However, they don't always understand how to value design because its attributes are not expressed in business terms. What are the benefits of good design? What are the true costs of poor quality design? How does design make a positive difference to the client's bottom line? These are the questions that architects need to articulate to their clients in order to rebalance the economic equation of risk and reward in professional practice.

"No project can be successful unless it is properly structured from the beginning, with clearly stated goals and identified challenges ... The idea of starting a project off right is so critical and yet so often misunderstood."

M. ARTHUR GENSLER

When you start your next fee negotiation, try asking your client this question: What are you trying to accomplish with this project and what is it worth to you to get it right? Then use the discussion to understand what value the client is placing on design and how you can best provide it. Explain your services in terms that the client can understand, using quantitative measures.

Sometimes the key issue for a client is speed, such as being able to deliver a new academic building in time for the start of fall classes. Sometimes it is budget — the ability to deliver at or below the prevailing cost for projects of a similar type. Sometimes it is design imagery — producing an iconic project that will attract tenants or that publicly symbolizes what is unique about the client's mission.

It helps to "unbundle" architectural services on a phase-by-phase basis and show the client what tasks are necessary to get the desired results. It also helps to put specific limits on the number of hours, design options, and total duration of the contract so that the client knows what they are getting for the money. One of the most important things to do in negotiation is educate your client about how their internal decision-making processes affect the cost, speed, and quality of the entire project.

If you are experiencing difficulty negotiating reasonable contracts, then chances are good that there is a communications gap somewhere. The glitch can be external (coming to closure on just what the client has in mind and what it is wort), or it can be internal (getting your staff to understand how to deliver the goods within the parameters of the contract). Either way, it helps to demystify. Put yourself in your client's shoes: What would inspire them to hire you? When you can answer this question in terms that your client will understand, you're on your way to a better structure.

Questions

1. Clients don't want to spend money on things they don't understand. How do you address this?

2. How can you use quantitative measures to explain the value of your services? Can you prove your value?

3. How will you make sure your clients are constantly informed about project status?

Redesigning Design Fees

Are you tired of design fees so low that you don't feel your firm can deliver great work? Tired of consulting expenses that increase your liability while eating into profits? Frustrated with clients who expect great service but can't seem to pay on time? If so, it's time to take charge of your finances and design a different way of doing business.

If money matters frustrate you, the odds are that you're distracted from doing what you do best — creating great solutions for your clients. It's time to stop complaining and get to work on the solution. Realize that form, function, and finance can all be viewed as design problems. And remember that it's in the client's best interest as well as yours to craft a financial relationship that makes sense for everyone involved — one that is easily administered and ensures an exchange of value.

> ***"I found that money was like a sixth sense without which you could not make the most of the other five."***
> SOMERSET MAUGHAM

Value is a two-way street. Take a moment and ask yourself what the client is trying to achieve by hiring your firm. What are you providing? What are the special benefits that accrue because of your participation? How can the design solutions you create bring support the client's business goals? Understand how this transaction looks from the other side of the table, and you will be in a position to approach negotiations with a win/win attitude rather than as a victim of circumstance.

If you cannot quantify design value for the client or distinguish your services from those of other firms, then you have placed your firm in the commodities business. This means that you are a price-taker — subject to fee levels set by the marketplace, not determined by your special skills. This is not an inherently bad place to be if you realize that your primary value is offering efficient, low-cost services. Your client will choose whichever firm can satisfy their needs at the minimum cost. In this case, concentrate on reducing your cost of operations rather than negotiating higher fees because your value lies in doing things faster and cheaper, not better.

On the other hand, if your firm has extraordinary design talent, special technical expertise, or substantial experience in a certain building type, then the task is to translate that into bottom-line results. Once again, look at this from the other side of the table. Here are some suggestions:

1. **Always express value in objective terms that can be measured by the client.** Show clients how you will get the project done sooner, that the space will be measurably more efficient or has a lower operational cost, or that you can increase their staff productivity in specific ways.

2. **Put the right people on the job.** Utilize staff who understand the client's goals and whose skills are suited to creating the right solution. If such people do not exist in your firm, consider hiring new staff or outsourcing portions of the assignment.

3. **Look for ways to simplify your accounting system.** Agree to bill for a set amount each month so that invoicing is automatic and payments can be approved routinely. Send separate bills for fees and reimbursable expenses so that any disputes about a few dollars in travel charges don't delay thousands of dollars in cash flow.

4. **Have a clear understanding of accounts receivable.** Know when to stop work or hold back on deliverables if payments are consistently late. If this sounds too harsh,

then reverse the incentive and provide a discount to all clients who pay within 10 days.

5. **Take pride in your business practices.** Make sure that they are best-of-class and that all of your staff understands how good management supports your mission to create good design.

6. **When you're busy, raise prices.** When times are flush, you need to store up a few acorns for the inevitable lean times that come with every change in the business cycle.

7. **Always reserve a portion of your revenue for retained earnings.** Continually invest in the improvement of your firm and your people. Your staff is your human capital, and the smarter and better trained they are, the more powerful your firm will be.

8. **Learn how to say "No thank you" to a commission if the fee is not sufficient for the job at hand.** Taking a loss on a project can be extraordinarily expensive. Don't let project losses be an unnecessary tax on your future.

The big lesson here is to run your firm with the same creative mindset that you apply to a design problem. What is the purpose of the organization? How does it function? How will it change over time? How can you creatively combine form, function, and finance? Think of management not as a chore but as process design. Good management is the lifeblood of any organization, so run yours accordingly.

Questions

1. How will you quantify the exchange of value with your clients?

2. How will you reduce your cost of operations without compromising quality?

3. How will you translate your expertise into bottom-line results?

CHARGING AHEAD — NEW FEE STRATEGIES

One of the most common sticking points between clients and architects is the question of what constitutes a fair fee. Because design by its very nature is creative, the process and outcomes are not always predictable. Yet clients, who often view the world through a financial lens, value predictability; they need to know what to expect. How much will the project cost? When will it be finished? What will they get for their money? These are questions that lurk in every negotiation whether they are stated explicitly or not.

By its nature, design is an exploration, and as the project proceeds there may well be changes to the program, budget, and schedule. These changes can be substantial. How is it possible to reconcile both the value and the uncertainty of design while still making good business sense for both sides?

First and foremost, it's important to recognize that every negotiation is fundamentally about an exchange of value. Each side gives something in order to get something. While it is tempting to think of this as a zero-sum game (I win; you lose), the unique quality of design is that it can actually create value for all parties concerned.

When you buy a product, the money you spend covers the basic cost of manufacturing and distribution plus an assumed profit margin. Cost of production is a primary price driver. However, in design, the cost of the architectural "product" (drawings, specifications, and models) often has little to do with the value of the service delivered. For example, when a client seeks advice about the development potential of certain commercial property, an architect may be able to render in only a few hours recommendations that are worth millions of dollars. At the same time, it is possible for architects to spend days on details that have little or no intrinsic value from the client's perspective.

Setting design fees can be a confusing and frustrating exercise for everyone. Sometimes the legitimate needs of the client (speed or cost control, for example) may be interpreted by the architect as antithetical to good design. Sometimes the personal passion of the architect will get in the way of the client's goals.

Over many decades, a generally accepted linear process for most projects has come to be recognized by designers and clients alike. The sequence is simple and relatively clear, progressing from the general to the specific: schematic design, design development, construction documentation, and construction administration. This appetizer/entrée/dessert mentality works to a point, but it ignores the strategic value that many architects are equipped to deliver but seldom articulate.

For instance, programming has traditionally been considered outside the scope of basic services, yet it is during this phase that the essence of a project's goals and values are defined, as well as its governing parameters of square footage and cost. A well-conceived program can save the client considerable time and money by making sure that the right project is being built in the first place. How much is such a program worth? About as much as a good map — the paper upon which it's printed is cheap, but its actual value is priceless if you happen to be lost.

With this in mind, approach fee negotiations with a designer's attitude — be creative when appropriate and definitive when necessary. Start by understanding from the client's perspective as much as you can about what it will take to make the project a success. Is it schedule, budget, or function; the desire to create an attention-getting building; or something else? It's a mistake to assume that your goals are the same as the client's going in to negotiations, but they should be in full alignment when you come out. Only by seeing the design process through the client's eyes will you be able to communicate how to address those goals. For example, do you discuss food in terms of taste, appearance, nutrition, personal preference, cost, or aspects of all five? Only after you have a mutual understanding of what is at stake is it appropriate to discuss cost. Before you know what something should cost, you have to know its value. Value is the ratio of cost to benefit, and it is the basis of compensation. Without a point of reference, there is no leverage either way.

There are many dimensions to a business deal, and money is only one of them. Terms and conditions, time, limits of liability, publicity potential, the prospect of future work, and good references all play a role in negotiations. If you focus only on the money, you'll rob yourself (and your client) of the possibility of a fee structure with a custom fit.

In today's competitive environment, there are many factors involved in both getting a job and doing a job. Some clients come to the table with a predetermined notion of what to pay, and others really don't know what they want or how much it should cost. Every situation will be different, and this is true even when you do multiple projects for the same client or work for government agencies that have established pricing policies already in place. Here are a few tips to demystify your fee strategy:

- **Do your homework.** Find out as much as you can about similar projects, their costs, and fees. This will help establish an objective point of reference for both sides.

- **Break the big job into smaller units and consider each one separately.** This is especially useful in projects that might have to undergo a complex public approvals process and for projects that are likely to last several years.

- **Negotiate for your consultants separately.** This will give you the opportunity to apply a mark-up on their services to cover your management time and the professional liability that you bear for their work.

- **Distinguish between fee for service and reimbursable expenses.** Reimbursable expenses have low intrinsic value to the client. Whenever possible, charge a reasonable mark-up to cover the cost of your cash flow.

- **When you cannot reliably predict how much a project will cost, charge by the hour until both you and the client have a better handle on things.** Hourly rates encourage both sides to be productive and efficient, and they take away uncertainty. You can convert to a fixed fee or a percentage fee whenever it is mutually agreeable.

- **Consider other forms of currency as a basis for compensation.** Stock warrants, stock options, reductions in operating costs, and fees based on the client's increase in profits or revenue flow as a result of the project are all options. This ties your financial destiny to the success of the project and realigns incentives on both sides. By being creative and redefining the risk/reward ratio, some firms are producing dramatic increases in revenues and profits.

A good business relationship between you and your client is essential to a well-run project. It will focus your creativity and will make billing and collections much easier and more predictable, increasing your cash flow. It will enable you to put your energy into what matters most — producing results. By approaching fee negotiations with this mindset, you are able to turn your client's attention from the question of, What is this costing me? to How can I get the best value? When both the client and the architect are thinking in terms of value rather than cost, then design fees will finally start to make sense.

Questions

1. How will you learn to negotiate better?

2. How will you set fees on value rather than cost?

3. How can your firm provide new, profitable services?

The duel becomes "The Duo."

DRIVING OUT FAILURE COSTS

All firms have the ability to control their costs better. Yet year after year, design firms insist on putting line items into their budgets for things that actually can cause failure rather than success. We call these budgeted but non-strategic expenses failure costs. Look around at your own operation. You no doubt will find failure costs embedded in your system; they are in fact quite common.

To be most effective, you must align your talent and resources to deliver results to your clients in the most cost-efficient way. Yet in many firms, the link between performance and profit is not appreciated by management. Ensuring the financial health of an organization must become a priority of the firm's leadership. Successful firms make it a hallmark of their culture. Lean management can be beyond smart business; it can be satisfying. Controlling costs means improved profitability, which provides the resources to produce better work. It's worth getting passionate about.

TIPS FOR DRIVING OUT FAILURE COSTS

- **Cut your supply budgets.** Every cost should be evaluated based on how it supports productivity.
- **Analyze technology costs.** Many firms are wasting money on both hardware and software.
- **Travel expenses can often be reduced without harming client relationships.**
- **Scrutinize your telephone and data transmission contracts.**

- **Go for functional, flexible workspace, then use your design talent to give it flair.** Show clients what you can do with a limited budget; it's great marketing.
- **Make smart decisions about employee benefit programs.** Benchmark against comparable firms, and review and adjust on a periodic basis.
- **Consider short-term incentive compensation tied to measurable improvements in efficiency.**
- **Review current pricing agreements with vendors.** Ask for discounts.
- **Ask your recruiting agencies for ways to bring down costs.** You may find a willingness to renegotiate agreements.
- **Use your website as a recruiting and communications tool.**
- **Control mailing and shipping costs.** Be certain that overnight delivery costs are reimbursable.
- **Rethink your marketing costs.** Focus on spending that actually improves your hit rate.

Above all, remember that every dollar you save can be invested in delivering better design to your clients.

Questions

1. What are the failure costs embedded in your organization?
2. What specific steps will you take to streamline your firm?
3. When should you consider downsizing to stay fit and healthy in an economic downturn?

Tips for Achieving Satisfying Profits

MARKETING

Avoid expensive design competitions. Design competitions are like speed dating: The attraction is based on first impressions only. Design competitions don't give you or the client the opportunity to think deeply about a project and give it the strategic consideration it deserves. They are also extremely expensive. Entering a competition can easily cost $100,000 or more, and this is equivalent to getting a new $10 million project at a 10 percent fee and making a 10 percent profit. Instead, invest that same money to improve your marketing in other ways.

Calculate your cost of sales. Cost of sales is the amount of time and money it takes to land $1 in new fees. Make sure your cost of sales is aligned with profit margins. If you spend 7 percent of your revenue on marketing but are only making 5 percent profit on the new work, you are slowly but surely going out of business. Evaluate your entire marketing program with cost of sales in mind.

Don't market by mail. Clients do not hire strangers. Responding to RFPs or public lists of projects without prior personal knowledge of the job is a very low-probability way to get work. Get to know the decision-makers in advance (including those in large government agencies). If you don't know the key people on the client side, look for other opportunities.

Nurture repeat work. Repeat business is by far the least expensive marketing you can do. Look for clients who are likely to have ongoing needs, and find a way to stay on their radar screen. Taking a smaller project to initiate the relationship will provide face time and position you for the larger projects when they come up.

Promote personal contact. Clients hire people, not brochures. Personal contact is the basis of trust. Lunches, dinners, museum outings, sporting events, or an evening at the theater are great ways to get to know clients as people. Become active in local boards or your clients' professional organizations as well.

Professional organizations. Active involvement in professional organizations is a great way to extend your network, learn new ideas, and build relationships. Don't just be a member — be a leader. Get on steering committees, nominating committees, and boards. Organize national meetings and preside at seminars. Visibility translates easily into credibility.

Provide innovative services. Help your clients obtain financing. Navigate them through the approvals process at city hall. Create alliances with other professional consultants, providing an expanded menu of services. Find out where the gaps are and fill them. You'll be surprised how this will expand your marketing horizons.

Unbundle services. Rather than negotiate long-term contracts, consider subdividing your services into smaller, bite-sized pieces. This makes it less risky for the client to try you out and easier for you to focus on doing a good job for a specific task. Try charging fixed-rate prices for specific services such as programming. Develop new rate structures (cost per square foot, cost per sheet of drawings, fixed average hourly rate for all office staff, etc.) that will make it easier and more predictable for clients to use your services.

OPERATIONS

Budget, then monitor. Finding out how much profit you have left at the end of a job is like driving down the street using only your rear-view mirror. Instead, establish key parameters of time and money before you begin, and then use them to guide your progress. Budgets are like guardrails — they are intended to keep you from going off the road. Use them.

Keep your project team intact. Changing personnel mid-stream almost always throws a project off balance. Instead, get the right team in place in the beginning and then leave it alone until the job is done. This builds commitment all around, and makes for better results. It's also a great way to teach younger staff about the integrated process of design.

Use state-of-the-art technology. Keep your software and your licenses current. Get the best equipment you can afford, and leverage its use on every project. Remember that machines are always less expensive than people, so maximize your staff efficiency by giving them the best tools.

Outsource. Many services provided in-house can be outsourced. Printing, model-making, specification writing, and even project accounting are a few examples. Keep your staff lean and totally focused on the job at hand. Hire out the rest. This can reduce management headaches and help you turn on a dime when necessary.

Encourage personal responsibility. Establish accountability at all levels of your organization and enforce it. Promote those who do well and reassign under-performers, especially at the senior levels of the firm. Do not tolerate a laissez-faire attitude.

Attack problems early. If you wait until the end of a job to confront problems, they will never get solved. Train your staff to get you the bad news as soon as possible when you still have time to do something about it. This is the only way to turn bad news into good news.

Read the contract. Encourage every key member of the project team to read the contract. In fact, insist on it. Knowing the extent of your responsibilities — and the client's — is the best way to make sure that mutual expectations are met. Understanding the contract terms will trigger better performance at all levels of the project team.

Be alert to additional services. All projects have some element of risk and the unknown. When conditions change, discuss the implications with your client. Changes can affect schedule, budget, scope of work, and design quality. When discussing additional services, always focus on the value to the client, not your own pocket.

PROFESSIONAL SERVICES

Link profitability and design value. Make the relationship between good design and good business practice one of your firm's core values. Good design is good business, and good business practice is good for design. If you can't demonstrate this argument, who will?

Get out of the vendor trap. Do your clients see you as a low-cost producer of commodity services? If so, change your strategy and find a way to provide unique value, something that no one else can do as well as you can. Then, even in a competitive market, you will have no competition.

Hire the best talent. This is always true. Get the best design and technical staff as well as the best secretaries, accountants, and support staff. Hire the best consulting engineers, and seek work with the best contractors. In the long run, quality is always faster and cheaper, and networking opportunities are a lot better when you have great people.

Delegate responsibility and authority. Now that you've hired the best people, use them to their fullest. Don't try to be a hero and do everything yourself. The more you rely on your staff, the more they will be able to do for you, and the more you can do for them. Everybody wins.

Use profits to promote design quality. Don't just focus on making more money — use it to improve everything you do. Get better space, buy better equipment, hire better people, do better photography of your projects, and so forth. When people understand that profitability makes a difference in design quality, they will perform even better.

Deliver what you promise on time. This promotes better time management, improves efficiency, and builds credibility all around. If you finish on time, you'll make better decisions, and your profitability is almost assured.

FINANCE

Tax yourself. Try banking 10 percent of every incoming check — without exception — in a special untouchable profit account. Even if everything else runs at a break even, this ensures a decent year-end result.

Mark up your consultants. You are legally and professionally liable for the work your consultants do on a job. Cover this risk by charging 10 percent to manage, coordinate, and deliver their work as part of your services. Alternatively, delete them entirely from your billing and have owners contract with them directly. (They'll soon see the value of the 10 percent markup.)

Charge "plumber's rates." If you don't know what a job is likely to cost, don't guess. Instead, use standard hourly rates until the scope of work and schedule are clarified. When in doubt, use "plumber's rates" — they compare favorably with those used by most architects!

Collect your bills. Every month, review your accounts receivable and call the clients who have not paid. If there is a problem, work it out. Unlike wine and cheese, old bills do not improve with age.

Link performance and compensation. Everybody in a firm knows who the non-performers are. Looking the other way doesn't help. Reassign them, retrain them, or help them find a new job, but don't let them fester in unproductive roles. Value your top performers with salaries, bonuses, and raises to build a productive culture.

Never shrink from asking for legitimate additional services. Most projects will generate about 10 percent in legitimate additional services, which is more than most average profit margins. If you ignore them, you are tacitly deciding to bill yourself for doing your client's job. Good clients will pay for the additional value they receive, but you have to ask first.

Create innovative fee structures. Stock options, stock warrants, bonuses based on schedule and budget control, or fees based on ongoing maintenance services are a few of the ways innovative firms are restructuring their fees. There is pressure on fees across the board even in busy times, so get creative.

Demystify your accounting. If your project staff doesn't understand your accounting system, it's not doing you much good. Discard the arcane and confusing spreadsheets and figure out how to explain the essentials on one piece of paper. Financial reports should be accessible to everyone whose performance will be influenced by them.

Automate time cards and billing systems. Computers can track most everything quickly, easily, and accurately. Set up your timecards and billing systems to be automatic, and make sure that everyone, principals included, comply. If you can't track it, you can't bill it or manage it.

Use computer tracking. For express mail, copying logs, overnight shipping, inventory supply, fax logs, and so forth, automate all tracking systems and integrate them with billing processes. Charge a 10 percent premium above cost, and capture that lost revenue.

Negotiate long-term discounts. Do you have favorite engineers? Would they be willing to cut their fees 5 percent in return for a guaranteed amount of work each year? Do you buy all your paper from one source? Would they be willing to give you a discount in return for guaranteed business? Leverage volume, save money, and improve service all at the same time.

Lose Your Losers

It is taken for granted in the design business that some projects make money and others are destined to be losers. This assumption is so ingrained that it's hardly given a second thought. In fact, working on a money-losing project is sometimes seen as a badge of honor: People can delude themselves into thinking that practicing until the money is all gone somehow makes for better design.

Great results come from doing things right in the first place, not from making repeated mistakes. Nonetheless, many designers still labor under a fundamental misconception about the relationship between design quality and profitability. Far from being mutually exclusive, they are actually mutually dependent — you can't have one without the other.

Common wisdom says it isn't what you make, it's what you keep, that counts. Accordingly, one of the best ways to protect profitability is by examining your loser projects. What went wrong? Why? Who was responsible? This is important because losers are double negatives — they not only rob the firm of today's profits, they place an invisible mortgage on your future operations as well.

There are several reasons that jobs end up in trouble. The first and most obvious is that the contract was not properly negotiated. Either you underestimated the amount of effort it would take to produce the job or your project leadership permitted the team to get off track. Both of these conditions are fixable. Negotiation techniques can be learned, and if you have chronic problems in this area, don't be too proud to get training; it will pay you back many times over.

If you have difficulty predicting a project's cost over several years' duration, try breaking the contract into smaller pieces and agree to set fees sequentially by phase. This will give both you and your client a way to establish value for your services as the project evolves, eliminating the guesswork for both sides.

As for project leadership, it's very important to provide clear and realistic expectations at the outset of each job. Make sure that appropriate staff is available, and establish true accountability for results. Without accountability, profit goals are meaningless.

> ***"We find ourselves in unprecedented circumstances — we need to rethink everything."***
>
> HON. RICHARD SWETT

At the end of each fiscal year, you can evaluate the effectiveness of project managers by tallying up how many projects of what size were produced, how many fee dollars were managed, what the average utilization rate was, and how many dollars of profit were generated. These measures are simple to produce and very telling. Don't try to manage your design firm without them.

If you have a problem project, sometimes the best you can hope for is to break even, but breaking even trumps a loss every time. Review the contract thoroughly to make sure that the entire team, including your consultants, understands the project requirements. Make sure you are charging for all legitimate additional services. Determine the minimum effort that will be required to get the job done with quality results, and don't accept the common complaint that it can't be done. There is always a better, cheaper, faster, and more creative way to work, and often these solutions only reveal themselves under pressure. Whatever it takes, stop the bleeding at once and don't let it recur.

Another common source of project losses is accounts receivable. If you have trouble collecting your fees, call clients directly and find out why. Sometimes the problem is a glitch in the accounting system; perhaps your billing protocols and those of your client don't match. This is not a surprise since many clients have unique payment policies. Learn what they are for every job you have, and follow them to the letter.

Bill separately for fees and expenses. Don't let a dispute about a $25 shipping charge hold up a payment of thousands of dollars in legitimate fees. If your clients are chronically late in their payments, tack on the interest and insist that it be paid. If portions of your bills are in dispute, get paid for the part that's not and resolve the rest as soon as possible. It's best for both you and your client that any misunderstandings are cleared up immediately and not allowed to recur. If your clients still don't pay as promised, it's time to part company. Instead of working for them at a loss, find other clients who value what you can do and are willing to pay fees that make sense.

Design competitions are another common source of losses that can be easily avoided. Except in extraordinary circumstances, where a reasonable stipend is provided or you have special knowledge or expertise about the project, competitions are a high-risk, low-probability way to pursue new work. They are also one of the worst possible ways for a client to choose an architect, since selection is based primarily on first impressions, and there is no time to develop a deeper understanding of the client's site, budget, program, and strategic goals. If you get the urge to enter a competition, even for a commission that you would dearly like to win, resist the temptation. Rather than roll the dice, use those same marketing dollars and the creative energy of your staff in much more productive ways.

Once you have cleaned up your losers, concentrate on changing your corporate culture about profitability. Make sure your staff understands why profits are important and how they will be used to improve the firm. Insist on timesheet compliance by everyone, especially senior staff. Get weekly timesheets at a minimum; daily is better. Conduct regular reviews by your project managers, identifying impending problems before they spin out of control. Address them right away, and you will eliminate project losses; allow them to go untended, and they will grow like weeds.

Take the mystery out of management by training your staff about budgeting, staffing, and delivering the goods on time and within budget. Make it clear that profitability is an integral part of the design mission of your firm, reinforcing the belief that losses are for losers. You will find that you attract better staff and better clients in the bargain. Why? Because fundamentally, profits are a measure of value. And if you can't create value for both clients and staff, then you're in the wrong business.

Questions

1. If you had to fire a client, who would it be? Why?
2. How can your contracts and documents serve your quality and profit goals?
3. What are the productivity speed bumps in your organization?

"You've really been a swell client, Ralph, but I'm afraid I'm going to have to let you go."

THE ANATOMY OF LEADERSHIP

Effective marketing, efficient operations, creative design, and prudent financial management are all essential elements of a successful firm. But what's needed most is leadership. Leadership is the ability to communicate your passion for excellence to clients and staff and then provide the means and methods of turning that passion into reality, inspiring others to commit their time and talent to the greater good. Effective leaders are downfield blockers — they clear a path so that others can run with the ball. And don't forget that leadership goes beyond the walls of your firm to touch the community at large. Good design is a value-added enterprise — it always produces benefit in excess of cost — and effective leadership is what makes it possible. Ultimately, you're in the leadership business. Design is your medium.

Embracing Change

Change is hard. It's human nature to cling to the familiar and resist the new. New things are untested and can be risky. New things require us to go outside our comfort zones and familiar habits. It's ironic that architects are experts at inflicting change on others but reluctant to embrace change in their own practices. Resistance to change invites stagnation. Here are a few of the signals:

1. **Creating ideas is easier than implementing them.**

2. **Talk of change is common, but old habits persist.**

3. **Goals are established, but there is little follow-up action.**

4. **Adoption of the latest technology is lagging.**

5. **The hours are long, but the work is not exciting.**

6. **People are focused on fixing the blame rather than fixing the problem.**

7. **There is little mentorship; young staff lack direction because they lack attention.**

Many architects do their best work in their later years; there's no need to grow stale. Buckminster Fuller, Frank Lloyd Wright, Cesar Pelli, and I.M. Pei are good examples. Staying current is a matter of attitude as much as ability.

We can learn to be elastic, receptive to new methods and alternate ways of doing things. As we change, we grow, and we help others around us grow as well. True professionalism welcomes change; it's the pathway to ultimate success.

> ***"The trouble with the future is that it usually arrives before we're ready for it."***
> ARNOLD GLASOW

QUESTIONS

1. What are signs that your firm is becoming stagnant?
2. What fears are blocking your dreams?
3. What changes are you willing to make in order to achieve greater success?

"I'm aiming for 'aggressively non-contextual.'"

Faster, Smarter, Better

The world of design moves at a fast pace; long hours and high stress are all too common. But faster is not necessarily smarter. What are the implications for firm principals who want to keep their organizations competitive?

Leading change is an ongoing challenge. Firm principals who are unprepared for change management often view change as the enemy. Whether you are prepared or not, you are functioning in an environment that requires taking risks and making choices. Bad choices can bring down the firm. Where there is choice, there is change.

Where does this put you? Are you leading change with entrepreneurial zeal or are you in the "ready, fire, aim" category, reacting to day-to-day pressures? There is a better way. Smart firms have found ways to enable positive, productive, and profitable forward vision. Their leaders understand that while the profession of architecture may be old fashioned in certain ways, the business of architecture is constantly evolving. They also know that even in a recession, design can be a growth business. Here's a checklist for becoming faster, smarter, better.

1. **Stop going to the same meetings and conferences.** Break old habits that are holding you back. Force yourself to spend more time with clients and get a better understanding of their major issues and concerns. Attend the conferences your clients attend.

2. **Articulate your vision — often.** Work on putting that vision statement into everyday language so that the people around you can believe it. Live your values: It's the best way to communicate what they really are.

3. **Be impatient.** Mobilize for action, and get others to join you.

4. **Be resilient.** Overcome the usual resistance and inertia. Deal with doubters directly and positively. There is no room for malcontents when you are in the process of building a better firm.

5. **Redesign your organization.** If you are to become faster, smarter, and better, the balance of power in the firm will have to shift. Recognize that change agents and the power structure are often at odds.

6. **Benchmark everything.** Monitor and measure everything in your organization that you can. Accountability matters.

7. **Be clear and compelling.** Meet often with your staff. Highlight the benefits of change in everyday terms. Use humor to reassure and motivate.

Change management is a key skill for 21st-century managers. Change can be risky, but it's also inevitable. It will make your firm faster, smarter, and better. Remember that any competitive advantage is temporary at best; you have to develop a culture of continuous improvement.

Questions

1. How are you a role model for leading change in your organization?

2. How are you communicating urgency?

3. What key benchmarks do you use to measure your organization's evolution?

Change and Stability

Architecture is a curious profession. Its products (buildings) are static, but its process (design) is anything but. While it is true that buildings are made of "sticks and stones" (and glass and steel and concrete), they are also made of a host of intangibles — ambition, aspiration, desire, conflict, and politics, to name a few. Permeating the design process, these intangibles are like a magnetic field whose presence is perceived but rarely understood.

Architects are constantly called upon to reconcile seemingly contradictory things: the clients' ambitions vs. their limited resources; the program scope vs. site constraints; the need to meet deadlines vs. the desire to do things right.

Eventually, the intangibles align, a design emerges, and the program begins to condense into physical form. A building takes shape. There are many ways to characterize this process, but it is often very hard for architects to articulate it in terms that their clients or the public truly understand.

Every project is unique — the client, site, program, budget, schedule, and team are never the same twice. Even people who work together constantly change as they gain experience.

As a result, it should come as no surprise that there is an almost desperate desire to find any system, protocol, policy, or procedure by which the design process can be codified and made more manageable. We not only have to fight the battle of communication and persuasion with our clients, but we also have to do the same with our colleagues, consultants, and contractors on a constant basis.

As a way of dealing with this organized chaos, firms often adopt policies and procedures that are intended to create some measure of stability. If only we could do things in a standardized way on a consistent basis, results might actually improve. There would be a higher level of quality, more efficiency, and improved profit margins.

Thus, we make charts and graphs and schedules and budgets and diagrams, and we hold retreats and concoct strategic plans, all for the purpose of establishing some measure of predictability. This is understandable but too often fruitless. The marvel is that we keep doing it without getting the results we are looking for.

The reason is simple, but it's hard to grasp. Stability itself is not stable because stability is process, not a state of being. Stability is actually a coping mechanism, an approximation rather than a destination. Sherwin Nuland, a surgeon and educator at Yale University School of Medicine, describes stability this way in *The Wisdom of the Body*: "A stable system is not a system that never changes. It is a system that constantly and instantly adjusts and readjusts in order to maintain such a state of being that all necessary functions are permitted to operate at maximal efficiency. Stability demands change to compensate for changing circumstances. Ultimately, then, stability depends on instability."

In other words, achieving stability requires constant adjustment. Like the rider on a bicycle, we can only keep our balance by continually moving forward. If we stand still, we fall over.

Successful firms are always monitoring their environment for signs of change and then reacting accordingly. Status quo is never good enough, even if the status quo is good. What does this mean for your practice?

- Do you know what your clients need not only this year but next year, too?
- Do you take the time to find out why you lose a project and then adjust your marketing approach to overcome the weakness?
- Do you constantly search for new management tools, such as financial software, that will enable your project teams to be better informed about where things stand?

- When you have trouble collecting timesheets from your staff or bills from your clients, do you do something about it?

In recent years, enterprises large and small have learned the lesson about change and stability, sometimes the hard way. There is scarcely a market, product, service, or an industry that has not been re-engineered, downsized, reinvented, or made extinct.

Because it challenges our familiar concept of what is right or good, change can cause a great deal of stress. But change is also exhilarating because it extends our horizon. Firms that cling to fond memories of their past successes and wish to relive the glory days are in trouble. Those that cherish those memories for what they are and look for ways to use past success as a springboard for a better future are much better positioned to navigate the inevitable bumps in the road.

Stability does not come from not changing. Rather, it comes from continual reassessment and a willingness to retain what works and discard what doesn't. This explains why even in the best and busiest of times, those in a position of leadership do not allow themselves to become complacent. The smartest among them always feel a little uncertain about the future. In their search for stability, they are always on edge. If you seek stability in your firm, you have to keep moving, remain alert, and stay nimble. Standing still is just a way of falling behind.

Questions

1. What part of your practice needs to change the most?

2. Are you asking stupid questions? (Smart people do it all the time.)

3. Are you taking enough risks?

Four Paradoxes in Design Leadership

Historians like to remind us that the only constant in life is change. Change is both wonderful and worrisome. In only a few short years, we have seen the birth of the information age, the globalization of the economy, and worldwide political disruption. What has gone up has come down. What once seemed impossible is now old hat. And what did not exist only a few years ago is now reshaping how we do business. Think back just two decades, before the commercialization of voice mail, email, smart phones, desktop publishing, the Internet, and social media. Indeed, it seems that change has become the dominant narrative of our times.

"Control your destiny ... or someone else will."
NOEL TICHY

Change can be a scary thing, but it is necessary and unavoidable. Without it, there is no growth. With change comes uncertainty, but it also brings new possibilities. Design is one of the last major industries to understand the value of marketing and branding and one of the last to embrace information technology fully.

It's time to get with the program. It's time to understand that change is not an enemy. On the contrary, it's where real creative opportunity lies. When old assumptions bump up against new ideas, interesting things start to happen. Such as:

1. **Charge less but make more.** Let's face it, the world is a competitive place, and that's not altogether a bad thing.

Competition breeds new ideas and innovation. These days, there is more pressure than ever on fees. So charge less, but make more by being innovative. Broadband your services, trade for equity rather than cash, reinvent your delivery systems to accomplish warp speed. If you don't do this, someone else will.

2. **Work faster but do a better job.** There are countless examples from other industries of how to do more with less: Microwave meals, ATMs and online stock trading are only a few. Why should design be immune? Instead of complaining, become an innovator and lead the way.

3. **Be high-tech but also high-touch.** Put off by technology? Can't program that smart phone? Get over it. Technology is a servant, not a master. Rather than drown in data, figure out a way to humanize it. Keep your life simple and focused. Invest in the best technology available. If you can't master it, hire somebody who can.

4. **Do better design by being better at business.** Good design and good business are not mutually exclusive. In fact, they are mutually reinforcing: You can't have one without the other. It's time to understand that creativity, innovation, and results are good business values as well as good design values. It's also time to understand that only profitable design firms will be able to invest in the technology, space, and talented staff that will keep them viable tomorrow. Want to be a better designer? Run a better business. And vice versa.

Designers are able to bring uncommon value to their clients. They can visualize problems and devise solutions that go beyond conventional thinking. They understand the fundamental relationships among form, function, and finance. They know the power of aesthetics. The very best are not bound by old habits — they think beyond what has been done before. In today's changing world, these are leadership skills as well as design skills.

Questions

1. What changes and trends are affecting your firm most?
2. How will your firm address the paradoxes in design leadership?
3. What will you be doing differently next month and next year?

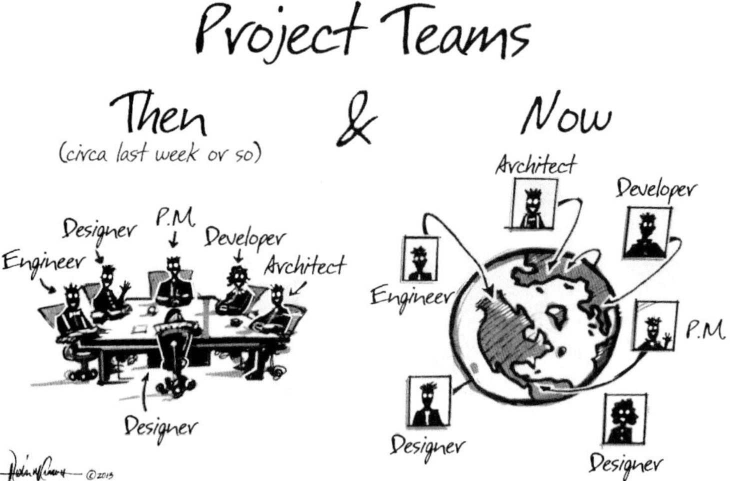

Solving the Right Problems

The need for smart thinking and assertive problem solving has never been greater. Yet many people in the design professions suffer from tunnel vision. Those who are effective problem solvers know how to ask the right questions, distill key information, and get to the heart of the issues. A useful resource for this process is a book by Ian Mitroff, a professor emeritus at the Marshall School of Business and the Annenberg School for Communication at the University of Southern California. In *Smart Thinking for Crazy Times: The Art of Solving the Right Problems*, Mitroff offers five key recommendations:

1. **Pick the right stakeholders.** It's almost always a bad idea to involve only a small set of stakeholders in formulating a problem.

2. **State the problem in multiple terms.** It is vital to produce at least two different formulations of any problem.

3. **Frame the problem correctly.** By using a narrow set of disciplines, design functions, or variables, you often address only the symptoms, not the real problem.

4. **Expand the boundaries.** Broaden the scope of every important problem beyond your comfort zone.

5. **Think systemically.** It's all too easy to focus on a part of the problem instead of the whole, to focus on the wrong part of a problem, or to ignore connections.

Above all, realize that problem solving is a team sport. The best way to create extraordinary value is to engage many minds with different points of view. Resist conventional thinking and be willing to consider counter-intuitive approaches. Being right is often the surest way to be wrong.

QUESTIONS

1. How do your clients describe your firm when you're not present?
2. How can your firm turn the five key recommendations into advantages?
3. How can you create a team-based problem solving culture in your firm?

Why Banks Are No Longer Buildings

Not long ago, banks and churches were the two most prominent structures in town. Banks were designed to symbolize security and safety. Their structures were intentionally conservative and even slightly intimidating, creating an air of respectable formality between customers and tellers.

Then in the early 1970s, a group of hotshot software engineers in Cambridge developed the electronic funds transfer system (EFTS). This was the first successful large-scale application of computer technology to the complex and arcane world of financial transactions. The ability to move money from place to place electronically was true innovation. The question was how to introduce the system to a reluctant marketplace so that it could be embraced by consumers.

To help answer the question, a special team of creative consultants was assembled to meet with the software experts and banking executives from the First National City Bank (now Citicorp) in New York City. The charge was to study the social implications of the new software to see how the banking industry might work differently, assuming that EFTS could gain widespread acceptance. The bankers knew the software was revolutionary, but they did not know what its ultimate effects might be.

The consultants included an architect, a graphic designer, and an artist. They were not experts in computer technology, banking, or marketing, but were chosen for their ability to understand and imagine the implications of change in complex systems, and then to give visual and practical form to how the new technology could be implemented. The financial guys knew that something big was about to happen to their industry, and they knew that they needed some pretty unconventional thinking to figure out what to do about it.

So the team went to work, holed up in a hotel with plenty of sketch paper, magic markers, and coffee. Ideas bounced off the walls, colliding and combining, disappearing and reappearing and finally coalescing. Various proposals were recorded, sorted, and rearranged on a gigantic roll of brown butcher paper. When the team was finished, 90 feet of ideas and sketches were presented to the bank executives.

The design team could see that the implications of EFTS were enormous. It correctly predicted the total reconfiguration of the banking industry. With the new software, checks no longer needed to be paper. In fact, money didn't need to exist at all. Banking didn't need to take place in buildings; it could be done anywhere. The software allowed any kind of financial transaction to take place 24 hours a day, instantaneously.

Within a few years, the first ATMs started to appear in bank lobbies. People were cautious at first, but as they became accustomed to the convenience and accessibility, the machines gained popularity. The number of banking transactions exploded exponentially. The number of tellers declined sharply, even as their productivity doubled.

Eventually, consumers stopped thinking about banks as a place to go and began to consider banking as a process supported by a network of financial services, available whenever and wherever they wanted. Banks as buildings began to disappear and became reincarnated as vending machines (and eventually as smart phones).

For designers, this did not mean the end of banks as clients. Quite the contrary, it opened up a whole new set of opportunities — renovations of bank lobbies, thousands of ATM centers, new large-scale data centers, and so forth.

What's the lesson here for designers? That technology crushes standards and that it can create previously unimaginable new paradigms. Some doors will close and others will open. Ultimately, it is the power of ideas that rules the marketplace. Design is what makes that power come alive.

QUESTIONS

1. If this can happen for banks, what does it suggest for hospitals, libraries, offices and retail centers?
2. How do your strengths become your weaknesses, and vice versa?
3. What really sells a product or a service? How do you know?

"Fork over the cash and nobody gets hurt."

Team Choreography: Making Best Use of Your Staff

Many designers cling to the romantic notion that great projects are constructed from flashes of brilliant insight. Creativity and inspiration are necessary, of course, but they are not sufficient. In fact, they are relatively useless without a lot of hard work to flesh out the details.

What design professionals can do better than anyone else is choreograph the creative and technical skills that are necessary to produce the desired results. This depends absolutely on communication and teamwork. Design students are erroneously taught that the road to success is paved with heroic personal effort and lots of caffeine. This is a misleading and harmful lesson. The truth is that success is a function of leadership and teamwork. Unless designers understand how to organize a team, the odds of professional success are slim indeed.

Ego and teamwork can be like oil and water, but this doesn't have to be the case. In fact, teams often benefit from strong egos — people who have a vision and are able to promote it passionately. That said, passion that is misused can be harmful and even destructive. In our professional careers, we have all witnessed talented people who just couldn't seem to get along with others and allowed their personal agendas to poison the project or disrupt the firm.

No project runs entirely smoothly. It is the nature of the creative process to be exploratory and to look at a problem from different angles in order to develop the best solution. Multiple perspectives can often lead to conflict, particularly if there is competition to win. If winning is defined as the difference between my way and your way, then it is a zero-sum game.

However, if winning is seen as producing the best possible project, then every idea, every suggestion, and every person is a potential winner. In this case, winning means being the person who can do the most good for the team. There is a world of difference.

People come with different sizes, shapes, attitudes, and talents. Smart leadership recognizes this and finds a way to extract the best from every person according to his or her ability to contribute. Though personal dynamics can be tricky, there are a few simple principles that, if followed consistently, will lead to better results for everyone.

1. **Separate the personality from the problem.** Everybody is entitled an opinion. However, a fruitful discussion focuses on the problem at hand, not on personalities. Decisions should be made on the basis of facts and outcomes rather than personal preference.

2. **Delegate appropriately.** Teams are based on the premise that certain members have better expertise than others in key areas. This is sensible, so act accordingly. Let engineers make engineering decisions so that designers can design. If your acoustical consultant makes a strong recommendation, odds are that there is a good reason for it. Listen to your experts — that is why you are paying them. If there is a conflict, develop an approach that no one has thought of before.

3. **Give clear, unambiguous directions.** In a well-organized team, each person has a defined role. First basemen should not attempt to play the outfield — this makes it very difficult to handle the bunts. It takes discipline to play your position so that your part of the field is covered, and it is just as important to keep out of the way and trust the other team members to play theirs. Let your team members know what you expect, why you expect it, and when you expect

it. Then hold them accountable. Reasonable directions that are consistently enforced will raise everyone's performance level and build trust in the group.

4. **Keep things in perspective.** Some things just aren't important enough to fight about. In academia, it's been said, "The politics are so fierce because the stakes are so small." In his classic book *Up the Organization*, Robert Townsend tells the story of a heated debate about choosing the color of coffee cups for the company cafeteria. Then it dawned on him that it would be faster and cheaper simply to make an arbitrary decision and change it later if need be. This is not to say that sloppy thinking should be tolerated, only that the level of effort invested should be proportionate to the value of the outcome desired. In other words, don't spend $10 to make a $1 decision. If it's not really that important, then don't worry about it; make a decision and move on to bigger and more critical things.

No project gets off the ground without a committed client, sound financing, multiple permits and approvals, defined budgets and schedules, legions of consultants, compliance with complex codes and regulations and, by the way, good design. It takes teamwork to manage all of this, and teamwork depends on effective leadership. Seen this way, leadership is, in fact, a critical design skill.

Questions

1. How will you train young staff to be leaders?

2. Do you give clear directions? How do you know?

3. If you are a good leader, can you also be a good follower?

Managing For Success: Synergising the Talent Around You

One of the great joys of being a designer is seeing ideas take flight and become real spaces and places. It is a magical transition, and one that requires both left-brain and right-brain skills, plus enormous passion mixed with tremendous attention to detail.

Because the design process is so personal, many architects find themselves thoroughly engrossed in it, and they have great difficulty delegating meaningful parts of the work to others. This creates an unintentional and counterproductive impediment to good design.

Every problem is multi-dimensional and complex and requires the blended talents of a wide variety of professionals, including architects, consultants, contractors, and clients. Ironically, it is the desire for ultimate control that is the undoing of so many designers, since no single individual, no matter how talented, can carry out a complicated job singlehandedly. Design is a team sport.

> ***"The greatest problem with communication is the illusion that it has been accomplished."***
> GEORGE BERNARD SHAW

The trick to getting results is to take maximum advantage of the talent at your disposal. Being a control freak is a self-limiting strategy, since everyone's time and attention span are limited. However, there is no limit to influence. Which kind of designer are you? One who's focused on control, or one who's focused on outcome?

We often seek control because we believe that nobody can do it as well as we can do it ourselves. A more accurate view is that nobody will do it exactly the same way we would. There is an important difference. Though all of us are talented, none of us is perfect. There is always more than one way to solve a problem and more than one way to get something done. If we allow ourselves a measure of humility, then we will realize that other people will have different (and sometimes better) ideas. If we are smart, we will borrow these good ideas because they will make us more effective.

If, on the other hand, we are convinced that ours is the best and only way, then we have the built-in opportunity to teach our colleagues and spread our influence. Either way, a dialogue opens up and the outcomes are enhanced. If we are too restrictive and controlling in our management style, then we deny our colleagues, our clients, and even ourselves the advantages of leveraging many minds to create the best solution.

Leveraging your talent requires delegation, and delegation demands a leap of faith that your instructions have been understood and agreed to and will be acted upon. Sometimes this happens, and sometimes it doesn't. More often than not, the "mistakes" our colleagues make in carrying out our intentions can be directly traced to inadequate or confusing instructions on our part. In other words, the delegation gap comes from us, not others.

How does this play out in day-to-day practice? To delegate effectively, you need to have the full attention of your team members. They need to understand your intent, motivation, and methods, as well as what you define as success. You need to provide room in the dialogue for discussion, debate, disagreement, and the new ideas that are bound to surface when different people look at a problem from various angles.

One absolute requirement for proper delegation is trust. You and your colleagues need to have a common goal uppermost in mind, and that goal is the successful completion of the project. This requires strong leadership because when people pursue different goals or agendas, confusion and discord are inevitable.

Good leadership sets clear expectations, establishes personal authority and responsibility for the outcome, sets the process in motion and then guides, but does not dictate, the process. If you are confident in your abilities, then making adjustments from time to time for unexpected circumstances is not a big issue; rather, it confirms your professionalism, self-confidence, trust, and sense of direction.

So explain yourself clearly, delegate effectively, trust yourself, and engage your colleagues both inside and outside the office. Abandon control in favor of influence. Being in control is temporary at best, but being influential is the path to sustainable long-term success.

Questions

1. What are your delegation disciplines?
2. How will you engage the talent around you without trying to solve everything yourself?
3. Does your staff believe you are organized and can delegate well? How do you know?

Asking For Help

If you're a principal, you're a leader. However, are you really exercising leadership, or merely authority? You get to make critical decisions about marketing, management, and design, and it feels great to be in control. You can decide which projects to chase, how to negotiate fees, who to assign to projects, how to handle key design issues, which consultants to hire, and who gets promoted in your firm. Now that you're in charge, what do you need most to be successful?

The answer may surprise you. What you need most is help. As a leader, manager, and mentor, your personal authority literally begins and ends at your own desk. It's useless unless you have others to interact with — people who understand what you need done and extend your influence by taking action to carry out your wishes. Leaders require followers (unless you enjoy talking only to the mirror!). In a very real sense, authority is like an electrical circuit — it carries no current unless there is a connection at both ends.

Exercising authority properly depends on three things not usually taught in design school: communication, humility, and restraint. Communication is critical. Without it, your instructions are sure to be misunderstood and improperly executed, creating frustration for all concerned. Humility is equally important. Show that you respect your team members, especially subordinates, so that they will respect you in return. Don't be fooled by the illusion of power. If you have to pull rank to get things done, it's like using too much salt — the whole dish is ruined. Use restraint. Power and authority depend as much on the receiver as the giver. You may get away with a little yelling and screaming from time to time, and it might even make you feel good, but ultimately, all it does is erode your professional standing both inside and outside the office.

The highest and best use of power is also the most subtle — it's called getting help. Getting help is the act of engaging others to assist you in accomplishing your goals. To get help, the first step is acknowledging that you need it. This is very tough for most bosses to do. After all, you've paid your dues to get to the top, and now that you've become a big cheese, you might be shocked to discover how powerless you really are without the support of subordinates. Surprised? Don't be. Whether you realize it or not, your subordinates are the only reason that you are a boss in the first place. Who needs a sheriff if there is no posse?

> ***"Everyone thinks of changing the world, but no one thinks of changing himself."***
> LEO NIKOLAEVICH TOLSTOY

Asking for help does not mean you have suddenly become a weakling. It only means that you have finally become strong enough to understand from both a strategic and tactical perspective how to make the best use of all of the assets at your disposal and to keep people fully engaged in furthering the firm's mission. Getting help from everybody all the time is the best way to keep things firing on all cylinders.

The trick is to get people to respond properly. Instead of just shouting out orders, make sure that your colleagues understand what you want, why you want it, when you want it, and what they can do that you are either not qualified or too busy to accomplish. When asked appropriately and instructed properly, most people love to help. They will eagerly take on new tasks and responsibilities if they know that their efforts will be appreciated. In the process, two things will happen: Your staff will become better helpers, and you will become a much more effective leader.

Power doesn't come from the number of merit badges you get but rather from your ability to solve bigger and more complex problems and to create increasing value for your clients, your projects, and your firm. Truly effective people understand this because they are less interested in the trappings of authority than how to exercise it wisely. Power misspent dissipates quickly, whereas power used appropriately compounds with interest.

The best way to get more power is to learn how to get more help. And to get more help, you need to learn how to be a better helper. Once you get the power, pass it along to others. If you doubt this, try an experiment. Spend an hour doing a routine task entirely alone. You'll soon realize that you're wasting precious time doing things that could be done better, faster, and cheaper by others. Then add up all of the things you have to get done in a single day, either at home or in the office. You will quickly see that putting yourself in a position to get the most help possible is the smartest use of your time. Then, and only then, can you exercise your influence in the best possible way. The wise use of power and authority is called leadership, and it works.

QUESTIONS

1. What are the differences among power, authority, and leadership?
2. How is power used in your office?
3. What can you do to increase your influence?

Choosing the Next Generation

Many an ambitious young designer has worked hard to become a firm principal, thinking that once this goal was reached, life would become simple. Adoring clients would flock to the door, awe-struck subordinates would implement every order promptly and without reservation, and consultants and contractors alike would instantly follow through on design decisions. The truth, of course, is just the opposite.

Becoming a principal means that life gets much more complicated. Rather than having only one boss at a time, leaders must answer to many. This includes not only external bosses (clients, bankers, reviewing agencies), but also internal bosses — the very subordinates that the principal purports to lead.

"Who must do the difficult things? Those who can."
JAPANESE RIDDLE

Why? Because being a firm principal means that you are responsible for the entire organization — you must find and secure work, hire and train the right people, create design that is both imaginative and practical, and stay on schedule and within budget. Make no mistake about it: Running a firm is not the same thing as running a project. It's the difference between playing an instrument and leading an orchestra.

Smart principals understand this. They learn how to identify the critical issues that need the most attention. They think strategically, finding ways to motivate others, and they delegate. If they are really smart, they also start thinking about the next generation of leadership from day one. Why? Because if they don't do this, they risk becoming the last principal the firm will ever have.

The best test of leadership is how well the firm is prepared for the next generation to take over. The landscape is littered with the carcasses of many once-proud firms that have lost influence because leadership transition was not a priority.

One of the most important jobs of a principal is ensuring an ample supply of talented, well-trained future leaders, at least one of whom will be able to do a much better job of running the firm than the current boss. Without an ethic of continually developing new leadership, the firm is in serious jeopardy.

How does leadership get passed from one generation to the next? Every year, a new crop of first-year students enters design school. Very few among them will emerge as leaders of their generation. Who are they? How do you spot the talent? How do you get them to work at your firm? And once you get them in the door, how do you get them to stay?

These are critical questions for any principal worth the title. Identifying, training and motivating talent is the single most important success factor for any firm regardless of size, location, or market focus. Why? Because a firm is only as good as its people. If you doubt this, try producing a project without a team: It's like trying to play baseball alone.

So how do you go about finding future leaders? First and foremost, you must be convinced that they exist, even if they are different from you. Don't look for clones no matter how tempting or flattering that may be. Each generation of a firm must respond to different pressures and opportunities, and it is very likely that tomorrow's leaders will need different skills. Instead, look for values. In any talent pool, find the top 10 percent — those who will find a way to rise to the top like bubbles in champagne.

The Ideal Candidate

The ideal candidate may not be obvious at first. Future leaders come from all backgrounds and with varying skill sets, but they do share some common characteristics. Foremost among these are curiosity and resilience, the ability to deal with people and hold their attention. Curious people never stop learning. They read, they attend seminars, they bug you about new ideas, they participate in professional committees, they develop new skills, and they bring their enthusiasm with them to the office every day. For them, personal and professional lives overlap and they find a way to integrate the two. They see their professional careers as a lifelong commitment.

Curious types tend to have good personal skills because they are interested in the world around them and what makes it tick. They have the ability to see more than one point of view at a time and understand how to deal with conflicting ideas. They recognize that everyone has something of value to offer and that the trick is to figure out what that might be and then put it to good use. They may be passionate or opinionated, but they are also tolerant. They respect the feelings of others even when they don't agree with them on every point. They know when to be politically expedient without compromising their core values. In short, they are inclusive, not exclusive, thinkers.

Regenerative Interdependence

The combination of curiosity, consideration, and commitment creates a leadership style that holds attention. When there is a project meeting, a client presentation, or an office conference, pay attention to whose words and actions actually carry weight and influence the outcome. Personal style is not the issue. Rather it is the ability to be an impact player, one who can articulate a sense of direction that motivates the group. It doesn't necessarily take great oratory to move a crowd — sometimes a quiet comment or a perceptive question will do the job just as well.

While some people might strive for attention, others will concentrate on getting results. There is a big difference. Pay attention to those in your firm who think clearly and produce the goods; those are the people that your clients will be paying attention to as well.

Once you have found your acorns, nurture them until they become oak trees. Challenge them with new assignments. Encourage them to get involved in community activities where they will meet many different kinds of people. Send them to seminars and conferences and expect a full report and a presentation to the firm when they return. Encourage them to take chances, and be tolerant of their mistakes. This will increase their confidence and humility at the same time — a most powerful combination.

Finally, teach them to teach others. Make sure that the ethic of passing the baton of leadership doesn't stop with you or with them but is part of the DNA of the firm, integral to the firm's DNA. Actively promoting the growth of new leaders from within and giving away power might seem like a dangerous thing to do, but in fact it is the only safe path to a sustainable future. Bottom line: When your successors are successful, so are you.

QUESTIONS

1. How are you preparing the next generation to lead?

2. How do you challenge future principals with new assignments?

3. Are you afraid of delegating yourself out of a job?

Criticism vs. Leadership

How do firms thrive? Why do some grow and others wither? What does it take to be successful in a constantly changing world? While we may hope for a secret formula or a foolproof organization chart or a magic key to unlock these mysteries, there is no mystery at all. The answer is simple and straightforward: Firms thrive because of their people.

A successful organization is one that attracts and retains talented staff and then provides an environment in which they can do their very best work. Good people love a challenge, they love to learn, and they love to work with colleagues who will push them to go beyond their comfort zones.

How do you go about making sure your staff is as committed as you are? First and foremost, recognize that each and every person comes to work with some kind of talent. (Otherwise, you would not have hired them.) As a leader, it is your job to unlock that talent and get it into gear. To do this, you need to be candid with employees about what you expect from them, how they can contribute to the organization, and how you see their growth potential.

> ***"Just as there is management unwilling or unenlightened enough to accept good design, there are designers who are only too willing to accommodate them."***
>
> PAUL RAND

More important, you need to be honest with yourself. It is not unusual for senior management to have an inflated self-image and subscribe to the notion that nobody can do it as well as they can. While this may hold true in isolated cases, it should also be a strong signal that you need to find and train somebody who can do a particular task better, faster, or cheaper than you can. Why? Leverage. Don't waste your time doing things that can be delegated. Instead, find a way of training and promoting people and helping them grow. This will free you to do a better job in the areas that really matter.

When you delegate, mistakes will be made — that's the nature of the learning process. Bear in mind that you can delegate authority but not responsibility. If something goes wrong, you are still on the hook, but don't let this stop you. Delegation most often goes awry when the subordinate did not clearly understand the task at hand. Another way of saying this is that the delegator — that's you — failed to communicate properly.

When you delegate, you are first and foremost a teacher. Because things are never perfect, you will be tempted to criticize way too much. The first reaction, a very human one, is too often negative (as in "That's not good enough"). When you react this way, you miss an important opportunity to demonstrate humility — a powerful teaching tool. Remember that there was a time in your life when you would have gotten it wrong, too. There was a time when you didn't know so much, made stupid mistakes, and had to rely on the help of others to get through the day. So lighten up. Share stories about your failures to make a point.

Criticism is often used as a weapon to demonstrate superiority. This causes more problems for the critic than one might realize. Unjust or excessive criticism only makes the critic look silly and diminishes credibility. Too much ranting and raving will cause the audience to tune out. Do you really want a leadership style based on intimidation? To keep your credibility high, use your comments to enlighten, not punish. And remember to give praise in public but to criticize in private.

Ultimately, if you understand how important your staff is to your success, you'll use your delegation skills carefully. You'll share your knowledge and experience generously. And you'll be astounded at the reaction. There is no leverage like the leverage of teamwork. A selfish or critical management style places a chokehold on the organization, but a truly wise leader takes as much joy in the success of others as in personal success. Know the difference between criticism and leadership. It will determine whether your firm will thrive or merely survive.

QUESTIONS

1. How can you share your weaknesses to strengthen the firm?

2. Are you a leader or a critic? How do you know?

3. What is your delegation style?

"I'll keep this meeting brief. The IT guys say the ROI on BIM is AOK. Any questions?"

Are You a Fish or a Thermostat?

Even in the best of times, the enterprise of design is fraught with challenges: how to attract the right clients, how to negotiate sufficient fees, how to hire and retain talented staff, how to make sure that projects are well designed yet still run on time and within budget. There are plenty of pressures and too many variables. However, success, like design itself, is not an accident — it is largely a matter of choice.

What are the critical ingredients of success? To some people's minds, marketing is paramount because in order to produce a project, the firm must first win it. To others, the key is innovative design. For the pragmatic, the production process matters most — the nitty gritty of getting the work done and making sure that all of the details are in order. Some believe that good management is most critical — making sure that all the policies, procedures, and numbers are in order so that things can run smoothly. The truth, of course, is that all these things are essential. It takes leadership to establish the balance.

Every person has a leadership style. Some see themselves like Teddy Roosevelt, leading the cavalry charge up San Juan Hill. They tend to be energetic, enthusiastic, and egocentric. They like to attract attention and inspire others, often measuring their success by how often and how much they win. Others are more like chess players — they survey the entire board and try to find a way to use all the pieces at their disposal in a coordinated and strategic way. They pursue a grand strategy and are willing to make sacrifices if the greater good is served. Either way, success depends on effective leadership.

Consider what success looks like in an aquarium. Some people might imagine themselves as a fish — brightly colored, exotically shaped, full of movement, and the focus of attention. However, the fish are utterly dependent on their context—water. A fish in water doesn't even realize that it's wet. It might compete with other fish for food or attention, but it really doesn't exert much control over its environment.

Success for a fish is really just a matter of survival. This does not depend so much on the fish as it does on the thermostat. Whatever the size, number, or species of the fish in the aquarium, the temperature of the water is actually the determining survival factor. A variation of only a few degrees either way will determine which fish will flourish and which will founder. While the power of the thermostat may not be obvious to the visitor or the fish, it is all-powerful.

Consider your own leadership style. Is pride of authorship important? Can you willingly (and gracefully) accept useful suggestions from others? Can you inspire action without getting in the way? Do you confuse criticism with leadership? Do you know how to delegate effectively, taking delight in the success of your colleagues as they strive to achieve their own goals? Can you provide strong and clear direction without stifling those around you?

Successful leaders understand the subtleties of these questions. They realize that in order for the fish to thrive, somebody has to work the thermostat. Design is a multi-faceted enterprise that requires the skilled contributions not only of architects but also of clients, consultants, and contractors. Even the most talented among us need a great deal of help to do a good job. By concentrating on the big picture, you can gain maximum advantage of all the talent at your disposal — especially if some of it's not your own.

Some people are made to be fish, and they require a support system for survival. Others are thermostats, more conductors than soloists. Which are you? Understanding your leadership style and how it affects those around you will allow you to make success a choice, not an accident.

QUESTIONS

1. Are you a fish or a thermostat? What would others say?
2. How can you make sure that all your "fish" stay healthy?
3. What is the right chemistry of criticism and encouragement?

"Say, don't I know you from somewhere?"

Don't Drop the Profit Ball

To evolve successfully, organizations must become better run businesses. It is their No. 1 strategic concern to adapt to change. Professional firms that survive and prosper are differentiated from others by the unique advantages they possess in marketing, service delivery, design talent, professional competence, and integrity. The management structure of the firm is the framework that supports and advances these qualities. Fundamentally, the competitive advantage that a firm has earned must stay fresh, attractive, and agile.

Managing a successful firm is a lot like being a juggler keeping five balls in the air. Four of the balls are red and one is black. The red balls represent marketing, money, people, and services. The black ball represents profit. No matter what happens, the black ball should never be dropped. Of course, most firm principals understand that they cannot exist without profit. However, the importance of profit often gets lost in the midst of an exciting marketing victory, a sexy design solution, or responding to an urgent client demand.

"The right thing to do and the hard thing to do are usually the same."

STEVE MARABOLI

Firm leaders cannot delegate profitability. Only the principals of the firm can be accountable. They must be the leaders and role models for the staff. Leadership is the very heart and soul of the enterprise. Far too many design firms are under-performing cash traps. Managing for success requires a strong business plan and a resolve to be an effective manager of people. Profits are sure to follow.

QUESTIONS

1. How will your firm stay fresh, attractive, and agile?

2. Leaders are responsible and accountable for maximizing productivity. What is your track record and how is it adapting to change?

3. How do you communicate your attitude about good business practices in your firm?

Leading a Healthy Organization

Times change constantly, and intelligent firms know how to stay nimble. They know that markets can shift dramatically. Land values will fluctuate. Capital investments will ebb and flow. Traditional opportunities to build backlog will decline. How do smart firms stay healthy? Here are five strategies to keep you organizationally fit.

> *"Norman Foster's most important characteristic, the one that won him the reputation he coveted, was his ability to change."*
> DESIGN INTELLIGENCE

1. **Craft a communications plan.** It is just as important as a marketing plan. Such a plan covers mission, vision, key messages, target audiences, techniques, schedules, budget, implementation, and monitoring systems. It addresses the need for communicating these things both internally and externally. Best-of-class firms know that a design firm is in the communications business.

2. **Structure your marketing budgets.** Advertise in the appropriate venues. Have a high profile at client events. Schedule public relations activities every year. Use creative methods to connect with key audiences. Successful firms are well positioned, enthusiastic, and ready to take away work from less aggressive competitors.

3. **Stay on top of technology.** Have a technology plan. Automate everything you can. Update your website frequently. Use the latest software, and keep your licenses up to date.

Make creative use of social media. Make sure that all staff have smart phones so that they are never out of touch with each other or with clients.

4. **Manage your overhead.** Keep fixed expenses down, and keep the work environment fresh, clean, organized, and energizing. Devise ways to do more with less. What you save on overhead can be invested in better design and better value.

5. **Have a leadership transition plan.** Running a successful firm is not just about cash flow, bringing in good people, getting work, keeping billable time up and getting bills and taxes paid. Firms need leadership that is energized, confident and caring, and is smart enough to pave the way for the next generation. This will empower the staff: they'll have tools and they'll have a coach. The staff should know they have a future with the firm, and they should look forward to being a shareholder.

A new world of design is unfolding at a staggering pace. It stands to reason that those firms with the best business skills and best design talent will have a big advantage. Firms should prepare themselves for what's coming. The market prospects will dim in some sectors and shine in others. Yet, design leaders can put the fundamentals in place and use their unique talents, skills, energy, and enthusiasm to design a better future for themselves.

Questions

1. What's driving change in your firm?

2. What are the forces resisting change in your firm?

3. Who are your next generation leaders?

PSYCHO-DYNAMICS

This is a story about office culture. A firm has exceptional talent and awesome projects. The potential for professional satisfaction is very high. Yet the firm also has an underlying weakness: the principals do not get along. There is a negative, permeating stress, an unspoken opposition that undercuts the firm's communications, morale, and leadership. The differences among the leaders have grown to be a lead weight that pulls down everyone in the firm.

> ***"Why is this firm dead? Why is it only an organization chart and a set of financials? Where do we measure its connections with people, with clients, with partners?"***
>
> DAVID FIRTH

Diversity of opinion can be a strength, but some firms behave in ways that allow diversity to become a weakness. A firm's intangible assets are based in the actions of the leadership. How well the people in a firm get along determines how well it performs in the world. Harmonious leadership is immediately apparent to all, and should be a hallmark of the firm's culture.

Ideological or personal conflict at the leadership level is corrosive, and erodes the firm's stature both internally and externally.

Yet it's also true that opposites attract, and that diametrically opposed opinions can spur new thinking, such as:

- **Exterior vs. interior** becomes **architecture plus interior design**

- **Design vs. business** becomes **design enterprise**
- **Design vs. construction** becomes **design-build**

Look for ways to combine binary opposites to create positive values that can drive the firm's culture. Exceeding expectations can be the new reality and make getting along the intelligent thing to do. Finding the unifying logic in binary opposites and creating harmony is one of today's most ignored yet powerful leadership differentiators.

QUESTIONS

1. Are your firm's principals aligned with each other?
2. How can you challenge the status quo in your firm without being oppositional?
3. What can you do to create more effective teamwork among senior management?

Design, Demographics, and Differentiation

All design firms, whatever their size, location, or market focus, have one thing in common: they are made up entirely of people. Like instruments in an orchestra, it is the blend of the people that determines the substance and tone of the organization. All people come from different backgrounds in terms of training, talent, skills, and opinions. It's the push/pull among these various factors that gives each organization its unique DNA.

Try this experiment. Pull five people aside at random and ask them each to describe your firm in a few sentences. Chances are you'll get five very different answers based on their position in the organization. Since not only your firm but everyone your firm deals with (including clients, contractors, and consultants) are also made up of people, it helps to pay attention to the powerful role that demographics and differentiation play in organization.

To understand your firm's demographics, sort your staff by age, sex, educational background, number of years with the firm, compensation level, work experience, and so forth. With this knowledge, you'll be able to track the stages of professional growth that all of them will go through in the course of their careers. This will help you deal with the behavioral aspects of managing people successfully and especially in how you put together project teams.

In general, professionals pass through four stages of development in the course of their careers: learner, doer, leader, and teacher.

Learners

The learners are the newly minted graduates who can't wait to change the world. They are enthusiastic and passionate, curious and inquisitive, and what they lack in knowledge or experience is made up by eagerness. The really smart learners quickly discover that there's a lot they don't know. They may be the lowest on the totem pole, but they have the most potential because their future has not yet been determined.

Doers

It takes about three to five years for people to pass through the learner stage to the doer stage. By this time, a person realizes that the real world is infinitely more complex than the ivory tower. Real clients have actual budgets and schedules, and project teams have to contend with dozens of complex issues in the course of producing a project.

Things aren't so black and white, and the passion of the learner is tempered by the political reality of getting things done in a group setting. During the doer stage, the employee usually concentrates on developing a specific skill set. Is he or she best suited to design, management, production, or perhaps construction administration? This is a critical stage because the path that is chosen will shape long-term career development.

The doers who successfully demonstrate competence will become leaders of teams, projects, and eventually, of firms. By this time, they have learned how to parlay their specific skills, which may in fact be quite specialized or limited, into much broader leadership qualities. As their judgment matures, they are seen as problem solvers — people who can deliver the goods when needed.

Leaders

Leaders realize that design is a team sport. They understand the power of leverage. They know that they cannot do everything by themselves and that they need the right kind of help to accomplish a larger goal. The willingness to seek and accept help is one of the hallmarks of a good leader, as is the ability to motivate others. Leaders understand the difference between strategy and tactics, and are able to use both to achieve the greater good.

Teachers

The leadership phase can last for many years, and some people actually stop growing when they have assumed a position of authority, mistakenly thinking that they have arrived. However, the truly wise do not stop there. Understanding the difference between control and influence, they realize that the greatest power of all is the power to shape the next generation. This is when they become teachers.

Good teachers don't stop learning, doing, or leading. They are concerned about developing the next generation. They consciously seek out promising younger talent, becoming mentors. If they are smart, they always hire people who are smarter than they are. Being both clever and wise, they realize that their success absolutely depends on the people around them. The influence of a good teacher extends throughout the entire organization from top to bottom, and the values that are transmitted are long lasting. It only takes a few good teachers to make a tremendous difference.

Charting the Territory

By charting the demographics of your firm, you'll quickly see what patterns emerge and where the gaps are. You'll instantly recognized the learners, doers, leaders and teachers in your organization. When you add staff, the demographic profile will help you hire strategically; you'll be able to match the strength of the candidate to the long-term needs of the firm.

The demographic analysis will also guide the management of your professional development programs. It will help your staff understand their individual roles in the organization and what the potential for growth is. Do you have too many designers? Not enough? Do the numbers show that you have too much turnover? Too little? Are you paying too much or too little for talent and experience? Has the time come to consider adding new partners or initiate ownership transition? These are only a few of the issues that demographic analysis will reveal. How you address them will determine your success.

Questions

1. How can you reinforce the four stages of professional growth: learner, doer, leader, and teacher?

2. Do you hire people who are smarter than you?

3. What does your firm's demographic profile tell you? Moreover, how does it differentiate you to succeed?

FIRE IN THE BELLY: MAINTAINING PRINCIPAL COMMITMENT

One of the myths about being an architect is that once you make principal, your troubles are over. As a leader, you expect loyalty and obedience from staff. As a professional, you expect a certain deference from consultants and clients. As a citizen, you want to be respected by the community at large. The truth, however, is quite different. None of these things happens automatically just because you get a new business card.

Some principals are working 65 hours a week and are required to market, network, manage and serve as referee, therapist, and parent. Many of those in ownership positions are asking themselves why they would aspire to such a position.

> ***"The idea is to assign yourself responsibility for being a motivator and an innovator."***
>
> I.M. PEI

In truth, making principal means that your life gets harder, more complicated, more hectic and more challenging. Your responsibilities have increased exponentially. Instead of being concerned about a single project or client, you are now expected to be a provider, creating new work for the entire office, mentoring the staff, and producing results for your clients, not to mention keeping the bank happy by covering payroll every two weeks. Being a principal is hard work. It is a position of great responsibility, and it carries commensurate professional, financial, and psychological rewards.

Becoming a principal is one thing. Maintaining the energy, commitment, and enthusiasm that got you there is quite another.

In sports, it is very common for a championship team to have an off season the following year because the emotional and physical energy that is required to win is even harder to sustain. The same thing is true in architecture. It is not uncommon for principals, especially those nearing retirement, to do a little coasting. After all, they've earned it. Shorter work weeks, longer vacations, and more leisurely lunches become the norm rather than the exception. While it is true that exceptional performance should have its rewards, it is dangerous for the firm to allow anybody at any level to slack off. This is especially true of principals because they set the tone for the entire organization. If the principals are not giving their all, who will?

How do you make sure that the principals in your firm continue to perform at the peak of their ability? How do you keep the fire in the belly from going out? The answers to these questions are complicated by the fact that design firms are too often run like clubs rather than businesses.

Partnership is not only a measure of professional achievement; it is also an affinity group. Each member brings different skills and attitudes to the mix, and establishing equal performance measures for all can be dangerous. At the same time, ignoring the metrics of principal performance is asking for trouble because when a firm loses its momentum, it is exceedingly hard to recapture.

Obviously, the most important time to discuss principal performance is when new partners are brought in. This is an opportunity for the entire ownership group to reaffirm what it means to be a leader and to renew everyone's personal commitment to the overall success of the office. The key is to focus not on what you get but what you give.

While every firm is different, there are some standards that can be reasonably applied to measure principal performance. The four critical success factors in any firm are marketing (obtaining new work), operations (creating and maintaining a productive working environment), professional services (producing great design), and finance (managing the money). Firms can be driven by any one of these factors, but each and every successful firm needs leadership in all four in order to thrive.

Normally, firms that are not sole proprietorships should average one principal for every 10 to 12 staff members and a minimum of $150,000 in net fees per staff. On this basis, a principal can be reasonably expected to produce about two million dollars in new net fees annually. In larger firms with more sophisticated marketing support, $3 million to $5 million per principal per year is an achievable goal.

On the professional side, principals should be expected to produce their projects on time and within budget consistently, setting an example for others. Performance can also be measured by the number of design awards won, the number of projects published, and the amount of repeat business generated by satisfied clients.

In operations, team building, training of younger staff, and attention to routine details such as managing time sheets and checking project reports are minimum standards, whether or not the principal is involved in direct firm management. Principals should always support firm management and be alert to new ideas about how to run the office more efficiently.

Finally, in finance, it is easy to measure project performance. How many dollars of gross and net fees were billed in a given year? What were the profit margins on specific projects? What is the average utilization of principal time? What is the ratio of new fee dollars generated per dollar of salary? It is easy to tabulate these results for all principals in the firm and then compare them on an annual basis to reveal trends. It's important to remember that objective measures of principal performance are for enlightenment, not punishment.

If your firm tolerates less than full commitment by its principals, everyone in the firm gets sold short. This includes not only internal staff but clients, consultants, and contractors as well. As principals near retirement age, their interests and value to the firm may change — it's perfectly understandable. When this happens, don't get mad. Instead, get creative about restructuring their involvement so that you can take advantage of what they currently have to offer.

Principal performance is the single most important requirement for overall firm success, so take full advantage of it.

QUESTIONS

1. How often do you evaluate principal performance in your firm? Do you support a meritocracy?
2. What are your performance benchmarks?
3. What steps will you take to increase principal productivity?

"Any questions?"

A Strategy for Winning

Making good architecture is a complicated enterprise. It requires not only the ability to conceptualize and give physical form to the aspirations of the client but also the management skill to organize and choreograph the activities of a multitude of diverse team members, each of whom has a special contribution to make. Ideas alone do not make a building. The architect's drawings and models are only the recipe — not the meal.

Like music, design depends on both objects and processes. A piano by itself does not make music. Without the composer to write the score and a musician to play the notes, a piano is just a piece of expensive furniture. So it is with design. The essential message of this book is that understanding why and how things get done is a necessary first step in doing them better. It's a complex business, to be sure, but that should not stop us from rearranging the parts and pieces for better effect.

James Watson and Francis Crick discovered that all the infinite complexity and subtlety of human life comes from only four essential instructions encoded in our DNA. The same principle applies to design. The possibilities of design are limitless, but they are based on just a few fundamentals. Any firm, regardless of its location, size, or area of specialty, needs all four to survive and thrive. They are:

- **Marketing:** Get the work
- **Operations:** Organize the work
- **Professional services:** Do the work
- **Finance:** Manage the money

Like the gears in a car's transmission, each of the four might be a slightly different size, but they are all interconnected and they are all necessary to make the car run well. Each part must be in sync with the others; a gear that doesn't mate properly with its neighbor can do real damage. For the design enterprise engine to run smoothly the gears must be the right diameter, properly aligned, and well lubricated. Even the smallest part plays a critical role. This is why there are no unimportant people and no unimportant processes in your design firm.

As the leader, your role is to be the downfield blocker, clearing a path so your staff can do their best work. Beware the temptation to focus only on the big problems. To be truly effective, learn to break the big issues down into smaller, digestible chunks — the speed bumps that get in the way. Then take action, one issue at a time. This is the surest way to establish a culture of continuous learning and continuous improvement in your firm. It's also the quickest way to unlock the potential of all the talent around you.

John Wooden, the extraordinarily successful basketball coach at UCLA, won more national championships than any other coach in the history of the game. He understood the power of simple lessons. The story goes that the first practice each year was devoted entirely to teaching the new players how to put on their socks and shoes properly. That's all they did — they put on and took off their sneakers over and over again until they got it right. Why? Coach Wooden knew that if a player developed a blister, even a small one, he would be distracted on the court, and this could affect the team's performance. He also knew that basketball is a team sport. It didn't matter who did the scoring as long as the team won the game. Did this mean that the UCLA team lacked stars? Hardly — they attracted the very best players in the country, they performed at the peak of their abilities and won national championships year after year. But it was coach Wooden's simple lessons that unlocked the potential in each player and made it possible for the stars to play as a team. This is the power of leadership.

When architects understand their potential as leaders as well as conceptualizers and designers, their influence will only increase. But in order to be seen by others as leaders, they must first see themselves in that way. They must understand how to apply the full range of their design skills, and this requires far more than just drawing lines on paper. They must also find ways to enable others to participate effectively in the design process, including colleagues, clients, consultants, and contractors. And let's not forget the public — the ultimate consumer and beneficiary of all this effort. The essential act of leadership is to unleash the power of the team. In this way, design can be embraced by all who are touched by it.

We live in a technology-rich age. Sophisticated software makes it much simpler to depict complex design options. Email, voice mail, and social media make instant communications ubiquitous. We all live cheek by jowl in an electronic village. There is software for project budgeting and scheduling to keep things on track. Exquisitely detailed models can be constructed from laser-cut parts or fabricated overnight by 3-D printers.

The profession is rich in new tools, but it still clings to an outdated self-image, and this needs to change. Architects are not the victims of tight budgets — they are the problem solvers who can show clients how to get the best value for the limited resources available. Architects are not the victims of building codes or zoning regulations — they are the interpreters who know how to unlock the true potential of any site. And architects need not be the cabooses on the development train — they can and should be helping drive the locomotive. When architects see themselves as the leaders that they can be and behave accordingly, there will be no limit to their success.

While this book contains plenty of pragmatic information about how to enhance your own design enterprise, its essential message is about attitude. We are fortunate to live in an age in which design really matters. From the smallest, simplest products like Post-it Notes to major cultural institutions like the Guggenheim Museum in Bilbao, Spain, people everywhere are beginning to understand the power of good design to make things look better, work better, last longer, and even raise our spirits. Winston Churchill's observation "First we shape our buildings, and then they shape us" is true, and it has been said that our buildings are the residue of our culture — the evidence we leave behind to tell the next generation what has been important to us and why. If so, it's clear that architects, engineers, and designers can (and should) be cultural leaders, political leaders, business leaders, and educational leaders. To do this will require a new way of looking at the power of design, as well as a new way of looking at ourselves. Essentially, this means that we are in the leadership business, and design is our medium.

The time has come to redesign design — to discard the archaic preconceptions that have hindered the effectiveness and affected the self-image of the design professions. The time has come to re-think our processes, protocols, and procedures — discarding the ones that don't work very well, and inventing new ones that will.

The time has come to take action, and this is where you come in. Benjamin Franklin wrote "All the great maxims have been written; it only remains to put them into practice." He was right. Everything you can imagine is possible. That's what design is all about.

Rebranding the A/E/C Industry

As we emerge from the current recession, it's time to put the days of budget-busting projects behind us once and for all.

There's an old adage in the A/E/C industry: Of the three critical aspects of a project (time, money, and quality), it's only possible to deliver two at any given time. Projects that run on time and on budget are at risk for quality problems, and those with high quality standards always seem to cost more and take longer than expected. Essentially, this suggests that at its best, the traditional design/delivery process can deliver satisfaction only two-thirds of the time. That's not an especially inspiring sales pitch. It's like going to a dentist whose advertising slogan is "It may be expensive, but at least it's going to hurt."

Design and construction are hugely complex and inherently uncertain. Each project is unique in terms of program, site, budget, schedule, and the client's design goals, not to mention the psycho-dynamics of team interaction. Design is a process of discovery; sometimes not just the answers but even the questions are unclear at first. Once designed, buildings require a tremendous amount of time, money, and coordinated effort to produce. Add in the effect of a dynamic market with constantly shifting costs and the vagaries of weather, inflation, and the availability of skilled labor, and it's a miracle that things work as well as they do. But is this the best we can do?

Recent studies show that the A/E/C industry is hugely inefficient. About 30 percent of all projects do not run on time or within budget, some 37 percent of all materials end up as waste, and more than 90 percent of clients believe that construction documents are not suitable for the purpose intended. Most clients approach their new building projects with a sense of anticipation mixed with dread. Clearly, the A/E/C industry has an image problem. It's time to change the brand.

A brand is an implied promise that expresses what the consumer expects when purchasing a product or a service. Brand equity is more than the thing itself; it also comprises a set of perceptions and assumptions, real or imagined,that define the entire provider/consumer experience. At present, the A/E/C brand promises cost overruns, schedule delays, quality problems, and conflict as standard operating procedure. This is exactly backward from what it should be. Rather than being perceived as a high-cost, low-value delivery system, the A/E/C industry should reposition itself as a value creation system. Properly understood, it's an industry that builds things of lasting value that make a significant and measurable contribution not only to the economy but to society at large. To get to the essence of rebranding, we need to attack the problem at both ends: technology and process.

When clients conceive of new projects, there is always a set of value drivers at work. Expanding an enterprise in order to offer new services or accommodate more staff, designing facilities to increase efficiency and productivity, or remodeling or replacing buildings that have outgrown their useful lives are all common themes. Clients will compare the opportunities at hand with the cost required to carry the project forward. It follows that the higher the imputed value and the lower the cost, the more compelling the project.

Establishing a firm set of expectations for something that has yet to be designed, bid, and built requires a certain leap of faith no matter how experienced the team involved, especially since the cost of materials and the impact of inflation will surely fluctuate over the life of the project. Schedules can change as well due to unforeseen circumstances, and delays always cost more money. But it's equally true that every building or remodeling project has significant inherent value. All too often the value is never clearly articulated to either the participants or the ultimate users. Why is a particular project being undertaken? What will happen as a result? How will this affect the people who live and work in the new space? Who will benefit, and in what specific ways? These are questions that pertain to each and every job regardless of size, location, or function.

Once the value proposition is made clear and measurable, it's much easier to assess the true cost involved. A careful analysis will often reveal that there is no net cost at all: new buildings actually create more value than they consume in resources, and they continue to create value for many decades. Buildings are not merely structures — they are generators of economic activity. In fact, on a cost per year basis, good architecture is remarkably cheap. The problem is that it must be paid for in advance, before the first occupants cross the threshold. This is precisely where the promise of effective branding comes into play.

Establishing prospective value is not that difficult; a wide variety of metrics apply. However, on the delivery side, controlling cost, schedule, and quality is systemic in nature and requires re-engineering the A/E/C process from top to bottom, including participation from all three major players: owners, architects, and constructors. Many established practices in the industry are outmoded and should yield to new technologies. Construction documents are a good example: They are time-consuming to produce, frequently inaccurate or uncoordinated, and even after completion must be substantially done over by means of the shop drawing process. Building information modeling (BIM) is a welcome alternative to conventional document production and addresses many of these problems. The bidding process is another old habit that is ripe for reinvention. Today, prices for labor and materials can be easily and quickly checked on the Internet. Ironically, conventional fixed bidding actually increases the overall cost of the project through added contingencies and by inviting change orders.

Outmoded contracts are a third example. In traditional practice, owners contract separately with architects and construction managers, but there is no direct contractual relationship between those who design the structure and those who build it. Yet standard industry practice calls for the construction manager to communicate with the owner only through the architect. Clearly, it would be much better to align the interests of all concerned in a single contractual arrangement, a process known as integrated project delivery (IPD), which is fast gaining traction.

The combination of technical innovation (BIM) with process innovation (IPD) is extremely powerful. Together, they offer a whole new way of designing and delivering buildings better, faster, and cheaper. With BIM and IPD, creativity and predictability are no longer at odds; in fact, they are mutually reinforcing. This provides a compelling new brand platform for the A/E/C industry, which is second only to health care as a percentage of the national gross domestic product (representing some $1 trillion in investment annually).

Other major industries have successfully rebranded. For example, the focus of health care is now as much on staying well (through diet and exercise) as it is about being taking care of after illness strikes. The energy industry has become a leading advocate for conservation rather than consumption. Even whole countries have been rebranded: China has been transformed from political foe into a valued trading partner.

The most effective way for the A/E/C industry to emerge from the current recession is through rebranding rather than waiting for a return to business as usual when the market picks up. How should this new brand be positioned? As an industry that produces high quality, sustainable buildings that require fewer resources to construct, use less energy to operate and maintain, produce fewer emissions, and provide healthier places to live and work. Delivered on time and within budget, of course. We should put the days of budget-busting projects behind us once and for all. We have the means and the methods to do things differently, with dramatically improved results. And best of all, it won't cost a dime. There is plenty of waste and inefficiency in the current system that, if redirected and redeployed, can pay for the necessary process innovation many times over.

In financial services, we take it for granted that our bank statements and credit card bills are accurate each month, right down to the decimal point. We expect our utility companies to provide power and clean water that is plentiful and cheap. At the supermarket, we can count on high-quality produce at low cost, even in the middle of winter. Why shouldn't we have the same level of confidence in the effectiveness of the A/E/C industry?

Questions

1. What is your firm's brand?
2. How do you articulate your value proposition for clients?
3. Do you take full advantage of technology to reduce cost and control schedule?

"Think he'll give us a refund?"

Design Goes Global

Over the next several decades, billions of square feet of new construction and renovations will take place worldwide. Is international practice right for your firm?

A devastating earthquake in Haiti. A disastrous oil spill in the Gulf of Mexico. Plumes of pollution from China migrating across the Pacific, courtesy of the jet stream. It seems there's no shortage of bad news these days. But there is a silver lining: It's become clearer than ever that the world is an increasingly complex and interconnected place. Issues of politics, economics, technology, and culture are deeply intertwined. Rich or poor, near or far, everybody, everywhere, has a stake in what's going on. It's precisely this sense of global connectivity that puts a premium on design.

Whether at the macro scale (clean air, water, and energy) or the micro scale (healthy ventilation and good daylighting in a school classroom), design thinking has become central to addressing the challenges of the age. Over the past decade, as more U.S. architects have ventured abroad, fees generated from international projects have grown at the astounding annualized rate of 30 percent. In return, more foreign-based architects are competing effectively for work in the United States, often getting plum commissions. Technology, especially building information modeling (BIM), makes borders porous. Outsourcing makes overseas collaboration fast and cheap. Huge international projects provide welcome opportunities for design firms as the domestic market continues to struggle with a spotty recovery. In a very real sense, design, like banking and finance, has become an international profession.

Is Global Practice for You?

However, international practice is not for everyone. It tends to be expensive and risky, with plenty of potential pitfalls. Some firms have made patient, long-term investments in selected key markets, such as China or the Middle East, and often with mixed results. Others have taken a shot at the occasional high-profile design competition: nothing ventured, nothing gained. Some architects are solicited by foreign clients because they have particular expertise in a specific project type, such as health care or biotech. Still others are taken abroad by their U.S.-based clients, who are expanding operations overseas and want to make sure that U.S. standards are followed. In each country or culture, there are variables to consider. Here are a few things to keep in mind.

Marketing. When soliciting business overseas, every firm needs a convincing value proposition. Think long and hard about what would cause a client to reach halfway around the globe to hire your firm. What can you offer that a local firm cannot? You need to be absolutely clear about this and make a compelling business case. When marketing work overseas, personal relationships are more important than ever. Business customs and tax laws differ, decision-making and approvals processes may seem opaque, and construction practices vary widely.

All of these factors should be reflected in your approach to marketing and business development. Pay especially close attention to local language and culture. It helps greatly to have people from foreign countries on your staff who can explain the subtleties. Above all, remain patient. International practice requires staying power; it is neither for the faint of heart nor for those without reasonably deep pockets.

Fees and finances. Fees will vary greatly, as will expectations about scope of work and the quality of deliverables. Very few foreign clients expect or need full SD/DD/CD/CA services as defined by standard AIA documents, so collaboration with local firms is most often the norm. When discussing business arrangements with foreign clients, make sure you understand specifically what will be expected of your firm as well as how the decision-making process will be handled. Bear in mind that the notion of additional services is generally resisted and that clients will frequently request multiple modifications to scope and schedule without offering any adjustment fee.

Speaking of fees, rule No. 1 is to get paid up front. Retainers are standard practice and absolutely essential if you expect to make any kind of a profit. It's not uncommon for the last invoice to go unpaid (and in fact, it's almost assumed in some cultures). You need to know your tolerance for risk, and you need to be willing to cut bait and walk away if invoices are not paid in a timely manner. Too many firms have been seduced by the glamour of international work only to lose out in the end: The projects do not get built (or the design is greatly modified along the way), and the final invoice is never collected. When doing work overseas, there is essentially no means to enforce payment other than trust and goodwill. Consider this carefully and proceed accordingly.

Staffing and travel. Obviously, long-distance travel is part of the deal. For many assignments, more time is spent on airplanes than in face-to-face client contact. Travel is time consuming, exhausting, and expensive. It also represents a considerable opportunity cost at home because when you're having a beer and watching a movie at 40,000 feet, you're not completing billable work at the office. Staff assigned to international projects need to have the personality, passion, and stamina to go the distance. Working across time zones often means keeping crazy hours, which can take a toll on personal and family life. Technology helps to a degree, but international projects cannot be handled effectively at arm's length; you have to invest face time.

Don't forget that the expense of constant travel — plane fares, hotels, meals, and Internet connections — add up in a hurry. In response, some firms have opened satellite offices. When doing so, pay attention to local regulations, licensing laws, and tax regulations. Above all, keep a close watch on cash flow. Once you get behind, it's difficult to catch up.

Outsourcing. Outsourcing has become increasingly common over the past decade. High-quality 3-D models and excellent computer-generated renderings can be had quickly and for a fraction of domestic prices. Some firms have experimented with outsourcing routine engineering and drafting, and others have gone so far as to subcontract construction documents entirely. Outsourcing is one way to keep fees competitive, but it requires extra scrutiny in quality control, particularly with regard to issues of code compliance. Remember that you are responsible for the quality of your documentation no matter where or by whom it is prepared.

When dealing with outsourcers, it's essential to be clear about what's expected in terms of deliverables. Allow plenty of time to review, edit, and finalize documents, and anticipate multiple revisions along the way. Make sure that any notes, instructions, or specifications prepared in a foreign language are carefully translated and double-checked for nuance and accuracy. That said, outsourcing can be an effective way of expanding staff capabilities without making a direct investment in hiring and training. Average blended billing rates can also make your firm far more competitive on both sides of the ocean.

Local associations. Construction practices can vary widely from country to country, and for this reason it is highly likely that an international project will include several local partners. Many clients desire their projects to be built according to U.S. standards, but desire alone is not sufficient. Access to quality materials, sophisticated technical equipment, and skilled labor should never be taken for granted. Specifications mean little if the local CM firm cannot deliver. Local codes and approvals processes are likely to seem Byzantine; it's best to have them handled by local experts.

When working with local firms, be prepared to stay flexible. Construction documents are not always adhered to rigidly. Modifications to the design can be made midstream, sometimes without your knowledge or consent. The authority of the architect may be questioned or even ignored altogether.

The best way to achieve desired results is to have a clear understanding about what is expected, from whom, how the work will be produced and checked, and who will have the final say. When working overseas, all too often the architect's only real clout is the power of persuasion. That said, associating with quality local architects can be an enriching experience for your office staff, who will be exposed to new ways of thinking.

Technology. When practicing across different time zones, it's critical that all key team members share the same technology platform. Set protocols and procedures up front so that everyone will know how to create, store, and retrieve information in an orderly fashion. Establishing a project website can be a great help. Using a common BIM platform is even better. Setting up teleconferencing capability is relatively inexpensive; it will likely pay for itself many times over in travel savings alone. Foreign firms tend to be tech-savvy. However, technology by itself cannot create quality results, and it's no substitute for well-defined QA/QC procedures. At the end of the day, what gets done is more important than how it gets done.

Changes in Store

As design goes global, it will change the profession in fundamental ways. For example, if a domestic firm provides SD/DD services but not CD/CA, the staffing profile will begin to reflect this. More designers will be required and fewer technicians. Eventually, if a firm lives on a diet of 100 percent overseas work, it will essentially morph into a rendering firm. This is not necessarily a bad thing, as the design concept will still be at the core of the firm's value proposition, but it does make for a very different office environment and work process.

Another thing to consider is the notion of responsible control as required by most licensing laws. If the designer lives in Los Angeles, the structural engineer is in London, the working drawings are done in Manila, and the CA is handled locally in Dubai, who's really in charge in both a legal and professional sense? If the notion of responsible control begins to fade as a professional value, it will have a profound effect on how the next generation of designers is educated, trained, and licensed. In that scenario, design will likely be perceived as much more of a commodity service; anybody can provide it from any location. The implications are huge.

In addition, as international practice continues to increase, relationships with construction managers will change. Overseas projects require a far more collaborative mindset than is common in the United States. Major CMs are often in a position to take on much of the technical documentation that is normally prepared by the architect. Once again, focus on your value proposition.

At the end of the day, whether your firm practices globally or locally, it's results that matter most. In today's complex world, designers have a great deal to offer. The built environment accounts for more than a third of all energy use and nearly half of all carbon emissions. Over the next several decades, billions of square feet of new construction and renovations will take place worldwide. The design profession is in a unique position to have a positive effect. Think big.

Learning by Design

Firms that embrace lifelong learning as a core competency are making a smart investment.

Take a look around. Whatever happened to videocassettes, 8-track players, and analog TVs? Once epitomes of high-tech, they are now quaint relics of a not-too-distant past. The world has changed at a remarkable pace, and it keeps changing. Like it or not, we can't help ourselves: Human beings are programmed to be inventive.

Never satisfied with the status quo, we seem to have a limitless capacity both to create and solve problems. There was a time when a 256-bit computer processor was considered state-of-the-art. Then Moore's Law kicked in, and megabytes gave way to gigabytes. Terabytes are next, closely followed by petrabytes. When nanotechnology really takes off and the promise of quantum computing is realized, who knows what the upper limit will be — or if there is one. This vast increase in computing capacity allows us to solve problems of baffling complexity at unimaginable speed. And this is just the beginning. It seems that as soon as we master a skill set or new technology, another springs up in its place. Consequently, the shelf life of expertise is increasingly small. True mastery in any field seems to have the lifespan of a mosquito.

With so much to learn and so little time, how are we to cope? All we know for sure is that the future will be increasingly complex and that it will require ever more sophisticated skills and tools. Is there any way to get ahead of the curve? How do we know what we need to know?

CHANGING RULES

Education is based on a pretty simple proposition. We go to school to learn useful stuff then apply that knowledge throughout our lives. The more education we have, presumably the better equipped we will be to cope with what the future holds in store. But new knowledge is created continuously. Indeed, much of what we need to know today did not exist when we were in school, and so of course it could not have been taught. Ironically, education brings with it a certain rigidity. The more we know, the less likely we are to adapt to new and different ways of thinking. The old joke is that a true expert is someone who knows more and more about less and less until he knows everything about nothing. Being "right" only works until the rules change, and they are changing all the time.

The key to coping with the avalanche of new knowledge is realizing that school is not a place — it is an attitude. Education will always be important, but it will be delivered in different ways in various settings using assorted technologies. Access to information is only one small part of the equation and one we've solved remarkably well. In fact, we're drowning in data. But data is not information, information is not knowledge, and knowledge is not wisdom. If we are to keep up, we need to re-conceptualize what it means to be educated and how we go about doing it. It's a constant process.

Great athletes and skilled musicians understand this concept. No matter how good they get, they still hone their skills every day. If they don't, they fall behind. They build this repetition into their routines as part of their lifestyle. It's how they keep fresh for each new contest or performance (without any CEUs required!).

A CEU IS A CEU

The notion of continuing education has been widely adopted across most professions, from law to medicine to education itself. The American Institute of Architects formalized continuing education unit requirements a decade ago, and most state licensing agencies have followed suit. The drill is pretty simple: sign up for an accredited course, log the CEUs, keep your registration current. However, the actual process for determining useful content is still surprisingly haphazard. Just about anyone can apply for course certification; the barriers to entry are not high. The usual sources include conferences, publications, professional associations, and seminars given by manufacturers, suppliers, installers, and consultants. Perhaps this plethora of sources this is a good thing since you never know where useful ideas will come from. But the system is still fairly reactive and disorganized; there's nobody telling us what we need to learn or what our priorities ought to be. A CEU is a CEU, whether it deals with process innovation such as integrated project delivery or a technical detail like flashing joints. The lack of a clear roadmap makes continuing education essentially a self-guided adventure.

Which brings up a question: Do all those accumulated CEUs actually lead to better-informed, more creative, more effective professionals? The metrics suggest otherwise. In the aggregate, the A/E/C industry is the second biggest segment of the economy after health care, but its productivity has been in steady decline for the past four decades. By most measures, the design and construction process is at least 30 percent inefficient (representing about $300 billion in squandered value every year). It seems that the more we learn, the dumber we get, despite all the continuing ed. What to do?

Education All Around

First, understand that learning is like breathing. We do it all the time without thinking about it. Every chance encounter, meeting, e-mail, or site visit can teach us something useful, if only we are willing to pay attention. This is especially true when we solve problems. While we are naturally inclined to avoid trouble, the fact is that we learn more from our difficulties than our successes.

The second thing to realize is that learning does not have to be confined to individual effort. There's no way that a single person can know everything (with the possible exception of Thomas Jefferson). Group learning exposes multiple points of view and enriches the overall experience. Very often students learn as much or more from their classmates as from their professors.

The third point is to choose your altitude. Some things are sufficiently understood from the 30,000 foot level (strategies and concepts) and some from 15,000 feet (processes and protocols), but for others it's important to get in the weeds, right at ground level. It's not necessary to know all the details all the time as long you have a firm grasp on the overall conceptual framework. Details can always be provided by additional research, committees, or task groups when needed.

A Learning Organization

With these three things in mind, it's possible to make your firm into a learning organization, one in which continuing education is deeply ingrained in the culture. The goal is to create an atmosphere in which new ideas are openly sought, presented, discussed, debated, and then adopted or discarded as appropriate. This kind of open source atmosphere energizes the staff at all levels, creating a buzz that drives the organization. Here are a few techniques that will help:

- **Publicize the problem of the week.** In design and construction, there's always an issue that needs to be resolved. Pick one each week and throw it out for discussion. What happened and why? How could the situation have been avoided? Given the circumstances, what is the best possible outcome? What should happen differently next time? Should standing policies or protocols be changed? Engaging the collective wisdom of the firm often results in surprising new answers to old problems; everyone learns something.

- **"Eat smart".** Everyone eats lunch, and most manufacturers, suppliers, or consultants are happy to buy sandwiches for a willing audience to attend a lunchtime presentation on a particular topic. You don't have to wait for an invitation — just call people who have something useful to say and ask them. Most likely, they'll jump at the opportunity to spread their expertise. Many firms have created lunchtime programs that are already accredited for CEUs, so this provides a double benefit for staff. The food-for-thought strategy is particularly effective when you're just about to start a new project. What will you need to know? What are the useful precedents? There are lots of sources with great information that are there for the asking. So ask.

- **Leverage conference attendance.** Many firms routinely send staff to professional conferences. The cost can be considerable, not only in travel expenses but also in non-billable time. But firms fail to reap the full benefit when people return. Make sure that the new knowledge gained is shared liberally by requiring attendees to give formal presentations back at the office. Share the conference handouts and keep a library. Three things will happen: You'll keep everyone up to speed on what's going on in the profession, you'll quickly learn which conferences are worthy of repeat visits, and your staff will get great experience making effective presentations.

- **Try a book-of-the-month club.** Pick a selection each month and form a group that is willing to read, discuss, and summarize the salient points for the rest of the firm. Put a copy of the featured volume in your reception area so clients and other visitors know what's currently being studied. (Maybe they'd like to join.) Add the book to your library as a reference for staff. Any subject that is relevant to your work is fair game. If you're really ambitious, write your own book.

- **Keep a CEU scorecard.** Do this not only for yourself but for your entire staff, and post it openly. When you consider the number of CEUs that are earned per year across the firm, it can easily run into the thousands. That's a lot of new knowledge. Figure out how to mine it, refine it, and distribute it so that it doesn't go to waste. You might consider giving special recognition or a reward (free attendance at a conference of choice, perhaps) to the staff members who accumulate the most CEUs in a given year. However, don't fall into the trap of thinking about CEUs only in terms of points. It's learning that counts more than counting what's learned.

- **Tap into your favorite consultants and subcontractors.** Ever wonder what it's like to install sprinkler pipe? Or how to calculate the average wait times for an elevator? People we work with every day know this stuff, and they've got great stories to tell. How does their business really work? Invite them over to share their world view — you're bound to learn a lot (especially how to avoid pitfalls). Storytelling is one of the most effective ways to transmit and store information. Make it part of your firm's culture so your staff will share their own experiences.

- **Grow your own experts.** Every firm has smart people, and most have surprising skills or interests. Find out what drives them. A few years ago, one office sponsored an employee art show. Staff exhibited various projects that they worked on over the years for their own pleasure, and much of the work was of astounding quality. Who knew? For example, one person in particular was an expert at making fountain pens from beautifully crafted exotic woods. Showcasing the skills and talents of your staff is a great way to endow your firm with a culture of curiosity. It also breeds mutual respect.

- **Produce your own conferences.** Every firm is good at something and has useful information to share. Try corralling this knowledge and setting up a mini-conference for an invited list of guests. What were the big lessons learned from your last successful project? What are the implications of new tools and techniques? Better yet, leverage the content by inviting clients, contractors and consultants to be co-presenters. Sometimes the best way to learn something is to become a teacher. It's also great networking.

- **Invert the pyramid.** It's tempting to think that older, more experienced staff have all the answers. Try flipping this around and inviting younger staff to showcase what they know. They may not be experts in how to specify plumbing fixtures, but chances are that they know a lot about social media such as Facebook, Twitter, and LinkedIn. Introducing new ways of thinking and honoring younger employees for the energy and insight they can bring to the firm is a great way to plow new ground.

At its essence, design is about discovery — solving problems in different ways with new tools and techniques. For this, lifelong learning is a core competency. It follows that designing learning into your daily routine can only improve results. Firms that understand this basic principle and weave it into their organizational DNA are making a very smart investment, one that will pay dividends for years to come.

The Softer Side of Technology

Technology places a premium on leadership and collaboration, demanding that everyone communicate in ways they never did before.

There's no doubt that today's increasingly sophisticated design technology, particularly building information modeling, is having a dramatic impact on the way buildings are designed, documented, and delivered. State-of-the-art professional practice now requires a significant investment in hardware, software, and training. Many firms have established a C-level position, the Chief Information Officer, to oversee the expense and complexity of acquiring, implementing, and managing the new systems.

Ironically, as more money is spent on technology, the shorter its lifespan seems to be. All that shiny new equipment and sexy software starts becoming obsolete the day it's installed. This is a great testimonial to the creative ability of hardware and software engineers, who continually dazzle us with ever-clever bells and whistles, but it presents a dilemma. The lifespan of technology is a mere blink of an eye compared to the lifespan of a building. In the years ahead, when we need to retrieve building information, will it still be accessible or will it be locked away in hard drives that are as obsolete as an eight-track tape deck?

New Ways to Work

Technology not only changes what we can do, it also changes how we do things. The traditional value proposition of architects has been to produce paper-based "instruments of service." These are handed off to the contractor for bidding and construction and are considered sacrosanct. Because plans, sections, and elevations represent two-dimensional abstractions of three-dimensional space, the concept of design intent was devised to cover the many gray areas that are not explicitly delineated. Design intent is like poetry (subject to interpretation), and it has been a boon to the legal profession, triggering too many lawsuits and raising insurance premiums for everyone.

A quick story will illustrate the point. Once upon a time at a fancy dinner party, the dessert course was suddenly interrupted by an enormous crash in the kitchen. The alarmed hostess hurried in to see what the matter was and came upon one of the cooks standing by a pile of broken crockery. "What happened here?" demanded the hostess. "Who's responsible for breaking my best china?" The cook, looking both sheepish and a bit defiant, simply stated, "No one was holding the plate, madam, so it fell."

Because BIM enables architects and engineers to portray concepts in three dimensions, the ambiguity of design intent is becoming a thing of the past. There is no longer a requirement for clients or contractors to be mind readers, as options can be fully and realistically depicted in both 3-D and 4-D format. In addition, BIM systems can be linked to various other software programs to drive the prefabrication process right on the factory floor, eliminating the need for an intermediate layer of paper-based shop drawings or submittals. This is an enormous breakthrough and is akin to what happened in the banking industry when ATMs were first invented — they allowed customers to plug directly into the neural network of the bank without the need to go through a human interface (the bank teller). This greatly increased speed while simultaneously reducing error. Most important, it put the customer in charge of the banking relationship.

That word "relationship" is at the heart of the matter. The power of technology lies not in the equipment itself, which is inert and useless without a user, but in how it affects human behavior. These new tools not only invite but require an entirely different approach to accomplishing the work. With paper-based documents, the question of primary authorship is relatively straightforward. An individual architect or firm creates the design concept, directs the consultants, oversees the drafting, and signs and seals the result as a specific deliverable. There's essentially a master chef in the kitchen (with a few highly trained assistants, to be sure) and a clear demarcation of responsibility between the architect and the contractor.

However, designing with BIM is quite different because it's a platform that accepts multiple inputs from many sources simultaneously. Indeed, the strength of BIM is its ability to integrate the contributions from a wide variety of experts and stakeholders (architects, engineers, consultants, suppliers, contractors, and yes, even owners) into a single coordinated database. In this way, BIM replaces traditional silo thinking with lateral thinking, linking together a lot of brain power with special expertise and diverse points of view. A well-managed team trumps individual effort every time. This may seem obvious, but it's as simple and revolutionary as putting wheels on luggage.

Control and Collaboration

The communal aspect of BIM begs the question of responsible control, which is at the very heart of professional licensing. In the high-tech world, there is no inherent requirement for physical proximity. Teams can be co-located in a single room or dispersed across the globe, as the recent trend toward outsourcing has made clear. When networked electronically, even small firms can achieve international reach. In this way, technology acts as a multiplier to leverage talent. It increases both market presence and productivity.

But who's really driving the bus on a day-to-day basis? That's why technology places a premium on both leadership and collaboration skill, demanding that everyone communicate in ways they never did before.

Because it is highly democratic, technology fundamentally alters the sociology of teams, breaking down barriers of age, experience, and rank. It's especially cross-generational. Anybody who's attempted to program a cell phone knows that the best approach is to bypass the instructions and simply ask the youngest person in the room how the darn thing works. The problem will be quickly solved with a few quick keystrokes and a bemused smile.

However, this comes with a note of caution. It's ironic that technology can both connect us and divide us at the same time. Case in point: In a typical meeting, many, if not most, of the participants spend much of the time using their smart phones to check messages, process e-mail, and text (sometimes to people in the same room). Technology allows us to multiplex — operate on several channels simultaneously — which dilutes our ability to focus on the issue at hand. It also affects how messages are formatted. Paragraphs are rarely lengthy, and long, carefully composed letters seems to be a lost art. These days, most written communications are a sentence or two at most, if not a tweet delivered in a maximum of 140 characters. So we're greatly condensing the way we transmit content and are beginning to develop a special language to do so. R U on 2 this?

Internet search engines, especially Google, have also had a profound impact on how technology impacts our collective thought process. The Internet is the largest pool of publicly accessible information ever created, and it's essentially free. It operates on a 24/7 basis and is not limited by cultural or political boundaries. Anybody can deposit information at any time (with varying degrees of accuracy!) and anybody can make a withdrawal, like a bottomless bank account. It has remarkably few rules and is essentially self-regulating. It can be used for good or ill. However, it's only useful if we can find what we need. (Imagine the chaos of a huge library without the Dewey decimal system.) The Internet is fast becoming the brain stem of the human race. If knowledge is power, then the Internet is the most powerful thing by far that has ever been conceived. It has transformed science, medicine, commerce, education, and even government.

With the advent of cloud computing, technology will take another giant leap forward. Systems are being developed that will essentially function as "design caves" with the ability to simulate a 4-D experience. A firm called SmartBIM is in the process of assembling a comprehensive library of BIM-based product icons (like an electronic Sweets catalogue) that can be easily inserted into design documents on a point-and-click basis. When voice recognition software is perfected, it will be possible to have a conversation with a client over a cup of coffee and translate design ideas immediately into architectural imagery on large interactive screens. The leap from the designer's imagination to the built environment will be short indeed.

New Perspective

While this may sound like a fantasy, similar scenarios have played out in other industries. Transportation is a prime example. A mere century ago, machine-powered human flight was in its infancy. Within a few decades, Charles Lindbergh crossed the Atlantic solo. A few years later, jet engines were perfected, and the sound barrier was broken. In less than a decade, from 1960 to 1969, technology was developed that successfully put a man on the moon. Today, no one thinks twice about boarding an airliner in New York and landing in Los Angeles a few hours later (well fed and well rested, if you're in business class). It should also be noted that air travel has become by far the safest and cheapest mode of public transportation ever devised on a per-mile basis. The notion of crossing a continent between breakfast and lunch while taking a pleasant nap would have been unthinkable to Orville and Wilbur Wright, but today it's as ordinary as riding the bus (and actually safer!).

Clearly, it was the advance of technology that allowed this to happen. But even more profound, the effect of the technology has changed the way we look at the world and the way we operate within it. It's entirely altered our expectations of what's possible and how we live (right down to the fresh Alaskan salmon that routinely appears on restaurant menus all over the world, which would be unthinkable without air freight). Technology has already engendered the wide-scale reinvention of many industries — financial services, manufacturing, communications, retailing, publishing, entertainment, and agriculture, to name a few. The A/E/C industry is hardly immune; although it is behind the curve.

In terms of design technology, we're just at the Wright brothers stage of development. We know that flight is possible, and we are able to stay aloft for a few minutes at a time, but we remain weighted down by our collective assumptions of how long things should take to build or how much they should cost. It's been said that if car manufacturers could match the productivity of the computer industry, a Ferrari could be bought for a few cents. The same basic principle applies (or should) to making buildings.

What's Next

Where will this take us? In the near term (three to five years), we can expect huge advances in next-generation BIM systems that will accurately and effortlessly enable us to create highly predictive models of architectural form, function, aesthetics, materials, construction logistics, capital cost, energy consumption, and ongoing facilities operations. Designing for efficient facilities operations and maintenance (which traditionally represents about 90 percent of the real cost of building ownership) could well become a new area of specialization for an emerging class of professionals.

Within a decade, nanotechnology will make possible whole new species of building materials — light, strong, easy to assemble, totally recyclable, and therefore cheap. We can also expect a surge in prefabrication techniques, which will enable construction sites to be as well organized and efficient as factories, with many routine tasks performed robotically. Waste, which currently consumes 37 percent of all building materials, will be reduced dramatically, saving hundreds of billions of dollars per year industry-wide.

Sound fantastic? Actually, these scenarios are fairly tame compared to the advances already made in aeronautics and computer science during our lifetime.

Where does organization and management fit in to all this? How should next-generation design firms be re-configured to take full advantage of the technology revolution? First, the easy part: Always bias toward acquiring the fastest processors and as much memory as possible, which will be needed to run upcoming software programs. Second, and even more important, pay close attention to the sociology of design, remembering that it's the people who drive the machines, not the other way around.

- **Create a tech-savvy culture.** Make it a habit to test drive new software systems when they are introduced. Invite industry experts to give in-house seminars. Send staff to professional conferences and trade shows to scout new systems. Make sure that the information they gain is shared freely.

- **Practice co-location.** When a new project starts up, organize the team in clusters or "campfires" of adjacent workstations. Make it a point to mix disciplines (seat architects next to engineers next to interior designers). Always have an extra desk or two for a visiting consultant or subcontractor to work alongside the team.

- **Organize by ability, not seniority.** Teams function most effectively when people work to the best of their abilities, like an orchestra. Don't expect the violinist to play drums. Value each person by the contribution he or she makes to the whole integrated effort. Make your project teams cross-generational and performance-based.

- **Change your metrics.** Don't be seduced by the rear-view mirror. Technology is a huge productivity enhancer. With it, more design ideas can be explored in greater depth in much less time. (If this were not the case, why bother?) Constantly challenge your teams to achieve higher and higher levels of creativity and productivity. Always seek to do more with less. Surprise yourself.

Above all, remember that the drawings are only a means to an end, and that all computers come with an on/off switch. The whole point of design is to make better places for people to live and work. Never forget that technology is merely the ticket to ride, not the destination.

Creating Value in the New Economy

Clients are looking for ever more creative solutions to their problems, but they also value predictability. Firms that can deliver both will be the big winners.

The ongoing fluctuations in the financial markets have made it clear that the economy has not yet returned to anyone's definition of normal and may not for some time. While the public sector struggles to digest massive amounts of debt without a significant rise in tax revenue, the private sector has been able to regain profitability through aggressive cost cutting, particularly by means of staff reductions, despite very modest overall growth in the gross domestic product. Corporations are now holding a record amount of cash but are reluctant to invest for the long-term, preferring to adopt a wait-and-see approach. As a result, unemployment remains high even while profits are healthy. This is instructive, and there are important lessons for the A/E/C industry.

Widespread staff reductions are causing clients to take a closer look at their overall space needs, correlating this closely with productivity. Few if any are planning for across the board expansion and most are seeking ways to reduce the average allocation of square feet per person. Operations and maintenance costs are also undergoing scrutiny, since every dollar saved enhances the bottom line. When new projects are approved, schedules are tight and budgets even tighter. Contractors are cutting prices to the bone, and professional fees are going down as well. On the bright side, there is an increasing appreciation by clients that space is strategic — that smart design can and should contribute to the bottom line by making measurable improvements in how organizations actually function.

In this context, design firms need to adjust their game plans.

In addition to the usual issues of form, function, and aesthetics (the what), they also need to understand the business aspects of any given project (the why and the how). Why is the project being undertaken? How does it relate to the overall business mission of the client? What are the financial expectations of the project in terms of return on investment? How can projects be designed to enhance the processes, procedures, and outcomes that underpin the client's organization? Far from being distractions or barriers to good design, these questions get to the heart of what drives client decision-making in today's economy.

As projects become more complex, design thinking needs to keep pace. Buildings are not just empty, inert vessels. They should be designed to support and enhance human activity, and so they need to be responsive to change. The added complexity requires participation from a wider variety of experts, and with this goes an increased demand for effective team leadership. The skills that designers need to be effective must be broadened and deepened. It's exactly the right time to re-evaluate the essential value propositions that design firms offer their clients.

In the past, architects were seen primarily as form givers, mostly concerned with program, function, and massing. In contrast, today's clients are much more likely to view built space as either a cost center or a revenue generator. (Some developers actually refer to buildings as "vertical product.") While it might not seem obvious at first glance, form and revenue are closely connected. But this is best expressed in business terms rather than design terms, which is something that most designers are neither equipped nor inclined to do.

The traditional view of professional practice is that "instruments of service" are what the architect gets paid to produce. Designers earn their fees by delivering discrete sets of documents (SD, DD, and CD) at pre-determined intervals rather than creating solutions to business problems. In fact, this attitude has been codified in standard AIA contract documents, where the phrases "problem solving" and "value creation" do not exist. And yet, that is what architects are really good at: solving multi-dimensional problems and creating new kinds of value in the process. Increasingly, the value is embedded in dynamic systems (such as mechanical, electrical, and plumbing), which have a huge impact not only in the upfront capital cost of a project but even more importantly in the long-term operations and maintenance cost. Yet traditional design thinking (and the fee structure that goes with it) makes no provision for this. Architects charge fees based only on near-term value (up to the date of substantial completion), completely ignoring the long-term value that in the real world dwarfs capital cost and actually increases over time, like compound interest. The benefits of smart design play out over many years.

New technology allows design professionals to study a much wider range of design alternatives more quickly and to analyze building components and systems with ever increasing degrees of accuracy and sophistication. Structure, lighting, air flow, water usage, and acoustics are just a few examples. This sort of analysis is not part of the standard model of architectural practice, but it should be because it's a good way of expressing design value in business terms. Technology also allows architects to display design options in 3-D and 4-D format, giving clients a much better grasp of what's possible and thus providing a better basis for decision-making. Technology can also be used to enhance both budget and schedule control as well as to model construction logistics. All of this greatly increases predictability, which is the holy grail for clients.

It's important to note that none of these technological enhancements detracts in any way from design quality. In fact, the opposite is true — technology allows a significantly higher degree of creative thinking and in much less time than traditional methods would allow.

Architects need to adjust their business models to reflect these new realities. Design is not limited to making new objects; it also deals with systems, processes, and procedures that in the aggregate support a new way of delivering the goods. When dealing with clients, consultants, and contractors, it's important to make these differences explicit so that they can be fully appreciated (and paid for). The accompanying chart illustrates the essential differences between the traditional practice model and the emerging model of value creation in today's highly competitive economy.

RETHINKING BUILDINGS

First and foremost, design professionals need to reset the deck, shifting the conventional perception of buildings as cost centers and replacing this outdated notion with the understanding that buildings are actually revenue generators. Also, buildings are not static; their functions and uses are likely to change dramatically over time, and they are increasingly interactive with users' needs and preferences. In this context, architects are much more than mere form givers; they are creators of built environments that are consciously designed to respond to occupants and enhance productivity over a long period of time.

Sophisticated computer technology now allows design professionals to model building performance in advance, tweaking the details as needed to achieve optimum results. There is no need to subdivide the process into the traditional phases of SD, DD, and CD; professionals can now provide an integrated continuum of services that comprises the full spectrum of design, documentation, and delivery.

Design is where the essential value creation takes place, and this includes both the aesthetic and business dimensions. During the documentation phase, expect much closer coordination with construction managers, suppliers, and subcontractors, up to and including co-authorship of the technical documents (even to the point of eliminating the need for submittals and shop drawings). Delivery (the actual construction process) will become much more efficient by means of increased off-site prefabrication of key components as well as computer-assisted tracking of materials, schedules, budgets and overall logistics during construction. Essentially, the construction site will become a mini-factory, enabling projects to be completed in much less time with a much higher degree of cost control and a minimum of waste. Eventually, standard contractual relationships, including liability insurance, will catch up with these new practice realities, as has already happened in other industries.

SHIFTING MODELS OF VALUE CREATION IN DESIGN

Traditional Model →	Future Model
Buildings as cost centers	Buildings as revenue generators
Buildings as static objects	Buildings as interactive, responsive to occupants
Architects as form givers	Architects as value creators
Conventional SD/DD/CD/CA process	Continuum of service (design/documentation/delivery)
Deliverables: plans, sections, elevations	Deliverables: 3-D & 4-D simulations
Professional silos	Integrated teams (O, A/E, CM, suppliers, subs)
CMs and subs isolated from design	CMs & subs involved in design
Architects not involved in means & methods	Architects as part of integrated building team
No energy use analysis	Energy use analysis becomes standard
No life cycle cost analysis	Life cycle cost analysis becomes standard
Two-party contracts (O/A & O/CM)	Multi-party contracts with performance metrics
Traditional single-payer insurance policies	Multi-party insurance policies
Litigation common	No-sue clauses common
Hard bidding	Continuous cost management
Shop drawings & submittals	Eliminated (embedded in BIM technology)
Minimum pre-fabrication	Majority of systems pre-fabricated
30% non-compliance for schedule & budget	100% compliance rate for schedule & budget
37% waste factor for materials	5% waste factor for materials
Schedules measured in years	Schedules measured in months
Cost-based design fees	Value-based design fees

The beginning of these trends is already evident. Building information modeling technology is fast becoming the industry standard for design documentation, as is LEED certification for sustainable design. Integrated project delivery, while still in its infancy, is producing consistently good results and is attracting more attention from owners.

Today's economic reality simply demands that more be done with less. This is true across the board, from industry to government. This is actually good news for the design profession, but it must be understood and communicated in no-nonsense terms, with plenty of metrics to support the argument. Once again, it should be stressed that this new way of providing professional services in no way dilutes the value of creativity. In fact, clients are constantly looking for ever more creative solutions to their problems. But they also value predictability; they want to know what they are getting, by when, and how much things will cost. Those who can deliver results will be the big winners in our highly competitive economy.

Perilously Provocative Predictions

A deliberately ambitious forecast of what's ahead.

Let's hop in a time machine and go back to 1990. The Internet was not yet commercially available. There were no iPods, iPads, or iPhones. CAD was in its infancy, and pen plotters were the highest of high tech in architects' offices. In 1992, Steve Jobs had been out of a job at Apple for seven years and would not return for another four. Larry Page and Sergey Brin were seniors in high school, and Mark Zuckerberg was just eight years old. Within a few years, a whole crop of Internet businesses would spring up like so many mushrooms and then die off just as fast. A select few, such as Amazon.com and eBay, would survive and eventually prosper, but it was far from clear at the time that they had much of a future.

Fast forward to 2012. Using a small device that weighs only a few ounces and easily fits in the palm of our hand, we can instantly access unlimited information, buy or sell whatever we like, and determine our exact position on the planet any time of the day or night. Had that sentence been written in 1992, it would have been considered outrageous science fiction.

What's Next

If past is prologue, what's next? By and large, the A/E/C industry has been reluctant to truly embrace technology and all that it implies. We still build things the old-fashioned way, one piece at a time. True, there's been some progress — glimmerings of building information modeling and a flirtation with integrated project delivery. As a whole, however, we're still mired in a mind-set that is based on instruments of service called construction documents, a bidding process that pretty much guarantees unwanted change orders, and a business model that habitually delivers projects late and over budget. (In other words, we may be inefficient, but at least we're expensive!)

Obviously, there's big room for improvement. Change is blowing across the landscape like a strong wind, and there's no stopping it. In the coming years, the A/E/C industry will look very different indeed. Herewith, a compendium of deliberately provocative predictions, intended to be slightly outrageous, all of which will eventually come true.

The End of Bidding (and Billing)

With eBay, Craigslist, and Amazon.com, we can buy pretty much anything we want, any time of the day or night, from anywhere around the globe, at the lowest available price, with just a few keystrokes. Airlines and hotels routinely adjust their prices based on fluctuating demand in order to maximize their return on investment. It's only a matter of time before the A/E/C industry adopts this approach to purchasing. And as long as we're getting rid of bidding, let's eliminate billing as well, with all transactions executed using debit card technology. Buy what you need, when you need it, for the best possible price, with zero paperwork. No bids, no bills, no bull.

Ubiquitous Bar Codes

In the retail world, bar codes have already revolutionized inventory control and point-of-purchase sales tracking. It's a very short conceptual leap to bar coding everything. Even people. Add the notion of a permanent built-in GPS chip or RFID tag, and nothing will ever get lost (bad news for thieves and kidnappers). On a construction site, the implications for ordering, manufacturing, shipping, storage, installation, site logistics, and waste processing are enormous. In an industry where 37 percent of materials eventually wind up in the dump, universal bar coding will save billions of dollars each year — more than enough to cover the cost of the technology.

Gaming the System

CAD technology, once leading edge, now seems positively quaint. BIM is a step up, but it's still in its adolescence. In a few years it will seem just as old-fashioned. Today, the gaming industry is at the frontier. It has shown us how to create a whole new universe of alternative places and experiences unencumbered by the constraints of the real world. Anything and everything is possible; we are limited only by our imagination. *SimCity* is just a start; there's literally nothing we can't game. Within a few short years, design by gaming will be the norm. Now take it a step further. Need to make a meeting on the coast by noon tomorrow? Stay home and send your avatar. Nobody will be able to tell the difference. Nor will they care.

Making Sense of Cyberspace

While we're at it, let's take gaming to new dimensions, literally. Even the most realistic computer games compress our 3-D experience into the two dimensions of a video screen. In the future, vastly improved technology will enable us to simulate all aspects of physical experience, including the five senses of sight, sound, touch, taste, and smell. This will allow us to explore, test, and validate design concepts in entirely new ways, and at warp speed. We've already seen glimmerings of this notion in movies such as Tron. Call it design by immersion.

Robots rule

Dishwashers, thermostats, and pacemakers are all forms of robots. Robots can be programmed to do our work for us, when and as we please, more efficiently and at lower cost than hired hands. The robotic revolution is just beginning. In the future, robots will be able to drive our cars, cook our meals, and handle our finances better than we can. On a construction site, robots will be programmed to perform a wide variety of tasks at all times of the day and night, with no complaints or coffee breaks. This will be especially useful for high-risk tasks. Sound fantastic? It's already happening. Consider 3-D printers, which, like Santa's elves, can produce exquisitely detailed models overnight while we sleep.

Nanotech Looms Large

Imagine a building that washes itself; glass that automatically adjusts thermal and visual performance for temperature, time of day, weather conditions, and occupancy; flooring that never wears out; and paint that can change color at will. Imagine buildings that digest smog right out of the atmosphere and metals that automatically bend themselves into a pre-determined shape as if they practiced yoga; clothes made of thousands of tiny programmable air bags so they are self-insulating in any kind of weather; and furniture that automatically adjusts to different body types and weights. Imagine super lightweight structures that are totally recyclable and walls that can switch from opaque to transparent at the flick of a switch or even move around at will by means of tiny motors. Sound crazy? So did the first ATM.

The Office Helmet

It used to be important to have a private office. Then the cubicle culture kicked in. Today, with a laptop, we can work effectively from any location on a 24/7 basis. Now imagine a baseball cap, made of self-powering solar-cell fabric, with a phone and camera built into the brim and a flip-down screen, like sunglasses, that provides ambulatory teleconferencing. Throw in a noise cancelling "cone of silence" for good measure, to ensure acoustic privacy on demand. Essentially, we'll be walking around wearing our own office space on our heads, able to talk with (and see) anybody we want. Need to have lunch with a colleague in Boise while you're in Boston? Just dial her in. In fact, with an office helmet, who needs a building?

Cloud Consciousness

Moore's law has proved to be uncannily correct. The math is inexorable: sooner rather than later, we'll be able to access all human knowledge on a chip, and it will be equally available to all, its use as natural as breathing. If knowledge is power, then the next generation will be the most powerful in history by far, with the cloud functioning as a gigantic supercomputer. This really levels the playing field. Got a problem to solve? Need something invented? Toss it out to the cloud, and it comes back done, in seconds, for pennies. The cloud will become the brain stem for the human race.

Talkitecture

With cloud computing, high-quality voice-activated software will finally become a reality. Imagine a conference room filled with high-definition big screens. As you describe the building to your client over a cup of coffee, the computer automatically translates your speech into 3-D and 4-D imagery. Want to change height, massing, material, or color? Just say the word. For extra effect, cue in a sound track. If you can say it, you can display it. (It's not much different in principle than using a synthesizer to compose new kinds of music.) This means that anyone who can talk can be a designer.

"You know there's an app for that, right?"

There's an App for That

Buildings are in large measure an assemblage of discrete components (elevators, toilets, windows, hardware, and so forth). Need to design a spiral stair? Size a duct? Calculate the shading coefficient on a window? Confirm code compliance?

Want to know how heavy a beam should be, or where to buy it, or when it can be delivered? There's an app for that. Point-and-click connections will key in manufacturers, model numbers, dimensions, cost, and delivery dates in a flash. Design-by-app will become as simple as checking flight status or making restaurant reservations on your smart phone.

BUILDINGS WITH DASHBOARDS:

When we drive a car, the dashboard tells us about the speed, temperature, gas mileage, travel distance, oil consumption, location (via GPS), and so forth. Why don't we "drive" buildings the same way? They may be static objects, but they are full of dynamic systems. Video displays in elevators already tell us about the weather, stock market, and sports scores; they could just as easily let us know about the building's occupancy, power consumption, water usage, temperature, elevator availability, and so forth. Informed people make better, safer drivers; the same could be true of building occupants. The obvious corollary is this: If buildings can talk to us, then we can talk back. The implications are endless.

If we look in the rear-view mirror, we are astounded by what has happened in a mere two decades, and there is every indication that the pace of change is accelerating rather than slowing down. The years to come are sure to provide even greater surprises. Making predictions is risky business, but here's one that will surely come true: In a surprisingly short time, all the predictions noted here will seem tame.

GLOSSARY

aggregation: Making otherwise scattered information accessible at single or multiple locations, usually via project management websites.

archetype: An underlying process that determines the form of imagery and symbolism, although not necessarily its content.

asynchronous innovation work: Remote software-based interaction allowing people to think, experiment, create, and contribute when they are most able (James Brian Quinn).

backlog: The amount of fee remaining in a firm at any given time. Also referred to as "fuel in the tank."

balanced scorecard (BSC): A measurement system that balances financial value and non-financial value, including design. A balanced scorecard is typically divided into a number, usually between three and six, of focus areas that have been identified as critical for the company. The focus areas are populated with indicators that are measured. Suitable for communication around and visualization of value creation. The term was coined by Robert S. Kaplan and David P. Norton.

balanced scorecard grid: A grid used for transforming the firm's strategy into measurable objectives, indicators and actions. The corporate strategy is divided into value creating focus areas of the balanced scorecard. Critical success factors are identified for strategic objectives within each focus area. Indicators are assigned to critical success factors to map the extent to which they are achieved. Actions that affect indicators are identified.

benchmarking: A continuous process of measuring and comparing outcomes, services, and processes with those that are "best-of-class." The 10 categories of best-of-class lead to "best practice."

best option: What generates the best outcome in the future. Relates to valuation of opportunities (future possible operations) (Timothy A. Luehrman).

best practice: What has generated best outcome in the past.

binary opposition: An analytic category from structuralism, used to show how meanings can be generated out of two-term systems. Meaning is generated by opposition. The binary opposition is the most extreme form of significant difference possible. Such binaries are a feature of culture not nature; they are products of signifying systems, and function to structure our perceptions of the natural and social world into order and meaning.

blueprint: A master plan for the realization of a vision.

book value: Defined as total assets minus total liabilities and represents the stockholders' equity on the firm's balance sheet. Book value is easy to determine but tends to understate the real value of the firm because assets are valued at cost less depreciation and no provision is made for the worth of the firm as a growing concern.

business process: Various related activities aimed at creating value which customers perceive and are willing to pay for.

buttress: A projection from a leader or a system of management that creates additional strength and support to an organization.

choice: "Where there's choice, there's meaning" is a basic precept in design communication.

client capital: The value of customer base, customer relationships and client potential. Component of structural capital.

client focus: The markets' and clients' perspectives on the business. A group of indicators and ratios describing the client base and relationships.

client potential: Relationships with new clients in established and new markets.

client relationship: current and potential business relationships with previous and present clients.

clients lost: The number of contracts lost during the year in relation to the total number of assignments on record.

cognitive dissonance: A state of disharmony, inconsistency or conflict between the organized attitudes, beliefs and values within an individual's cognitive system.

commercial competence: Designers' ability to collaborate with clients and other consulting partners in value creating constellations.

community of practice: A basis for collaboration in the execution of real work, based on a common sense of purpose and a real need to know what each other knows. Developed by the Institute of Learning.

competence: Encompasses knowledge, will, and skill, including professional, social, and commercial ability.

competence alliance: A network of individuals/units/firms with various competence profiles.

competence network: Organized network with a common goal of individual competence development within a certain area. Activities include sharing of information, ideas and experiences as well as a transfer of knowledge to members of the network. The core of the network is the interpersonal connections.

consensus: A term used to imply shared agreement.

contactivity: A meeting that goes beyond connectivity and creates both contact and meeting of minds leading to activity (Leif Edvinsson).

core competence: Competence that is of strategic importance for the firm's business logic.

core process: Value creating processes of strategic importance for the firm's business logic. Sometimes thought of as a "trade secret" because of unique value that some firms' processes contain.

corporate (organizational) memory: The organization's ability to transform and add experiences to the structural capital. The ability to recall, remembering what is needed when it is needed; Animated memory that supports the business processes: without stifling the innovation (Bob Johansen).

culture: The combined sum of the individual opinions, shared mindsets, values and norms (Hubert Saint-Onge). A component of organizational capital.

Economic Value Added (EVA)™: Value added that an operation generates during a certain period after deducting all costs, including capital costs for all invested or borrowed capital. Trademark owned by Stern Stewart & Company.

empiricism: An approach emphasizing the importance of observable, measurable and quantifiable evidence.

Employee Stock Ownership Plan (ESOP): An Employee Stock Ownership Plan is a type of employee benefit called a "defined contribution" plan. A fixed schedule of benefits determines what each employee will receive upon retirement, and this amount is guaranteed under the terms of the plan. The employer is then obligated to contribute what is necessary to provide these benefits.

fair market value: The price at which a business would change hands between a willing buyer and a willing seller, both being adequately informed of the relevant facts, and neither being under any compulsion to buy or sell.

fair value: Certain state statutes define value for the purpose of establishing dissenting stockholder rights. These definitions are much less clear, typically using the term "fair value" instead of "fair market value." There is no universally accepted definition of fair value. This leads to litigation on dissenting stockholder rights issues.

Gestalt: The recognition of wholeness and overall form rather than of individual component elements. An understanding of all the parts within any given structure will not provide a complete understanding of the total structure. Instead, meaning derives from the interrelationships of those parts, and of each part of the whole.

globalization: The growth and acceleration of economic and cultural networks which operate on a worldwide scale and basis.

goodwill: There are generally two types of goodwill: personal goodwill (often referred to as professional goodwill) and business goodwill (often referred to as practice goodwill). Personal goodwill is the goodwill associated with the individual. Business goodwill is the value of a business over and above its identifiable assets less liabilities.

human capital: The accumulated value of investments in employee training, competence, and future. The term focuses on the value of what the individual can produce; human capital thus encompasses individual value in an economic sense (Gary S. Becker). Can be described as the employees' competence, relationship ability and values. Work on human capital often focuses on transforming individual into collective competence and more enduring organizational capital.

human capital index: An index that indicates employees' attitudes regarding competence, motivation, responsibility and authority, cooperation and organizational efficiency.

human focus: The employee perspective. A group of indicators and ratios describing individual and collective competence and capabilities.

IC: For intellectual capital. The consolidation of structural capital and human capital, indicating future earnings capability. A concept developed by Leif Edvinsson.

IC leadership: The bridge between human capital, organizational capital and customer capital. Creates congruence and multiplicative effects between strategies, structures, systems and cultures in the business, market and operating environment in which an organization works.

icon/iconic: Type of sign in which there is a marked physical or perceptual resemblance between the signifier and that for which it stands.

image: Commonly means a public impression created to appeal to the audience. It may be false or authentic, and is part of brand repute.

indicator: A measurement that visualizes a certain aspect of the organization that has been identified having an impact as a key success factor. Indicators have the purpose of indicating a certain development and not to describe a target value.

information management (IM): The process of synthesizing, structuring and making information accessible.

innovation: The capacity to create a new idea or way. There are two types of innovation: one in the form of improving already existing products or services and the other in the form of creating totally new products and services. Innovation often includes three stages: invention, translation and commercialization. Innovative firms have reason to charge higher fees.

intellectual asset: Intangible asset more closely related to brain power. Sometimes referred to as applied brilliance. It is a leadership quality but does not stand up well on its own in terms of leadership.

intellectual property: Intellectual assets that qualify for legal and commercial protection, i.e. patents, trademarks, copyrights, and trade secrets.

invention: Power of inventing or being invented. Ingenuity or creativity. Something originating in an experiment.

key performance indicator (KPI): A particular ratio or characteristic used to measure output or outcome. KPIs are "metrics of value."

key success factor (KSF): Factors that are essential in order to achieve the strategic objectives/vision statements. Critical value drivers. Best-of-class firms understand how KSFs differentiate them from traditional firms.

knowledge: Information that has value in the interaction with human capital. The ability people have to use information to solve complex problems and adapt to change. The individual ability to master the unknown. The ability to act (Karl Erik Sveiby). Knowledge can be classified as explicit or tacit (Ikujiro Nonaka).

knowledge cafe: A metaphor alluding to the fact that knowledge workers might not work at the office but in an open inviting environment, like a café. A knowledge recipe for the workplace of tomorrow for knowledge workers.

knowledge exchange: The new arena on Internet for exchange of knowledge assets.

knowledge flows: A firm's internal and external flows of knowledge.

knowledge management (KM): Knowledge management includes managing information (explicit/recorded knowledge); managing processes (embedded knowledge); managing people (tacit knowledge); managing innovation (knowledge conversion); and managing assets (intellectual capital) (David Skyrme, Nick Willard). Keeping data that have been aggregated orderly, and analyzing them for trends and other useful insights. Also known as "content management."

knowledge strategy: The organization's strategy for optimizing the internal and external knowledge as well as flows in order to grow intellectual capital.

leading indicator: Early warning proactive indicators. In a cause/effect relationship, leading indicators cause an effect on the lagging indicators. An indicator can be leading in its nature in one situation, but lagging in another.

learning organization: A learning organization is one that enables frequent knowledge interaction and capitalizes on new knowledge created in these interactions. A learning organization is more than an "organization that learns." Building a learning organization means changing the company's culture, structure, processes, leadership and forms of cooperation. The term is coined by Peter M. Senge.

market price: The price at which seller and buyer are ready and willing to commit.

market value added (MVA): The difference between market value and invested capital. Sometimes measured as market capitalization less adjusted shareholders' equity. Also corresponds to static intellectual capital, excluding expectation value.

objectivity: An analytic approach that is supposedly characterized by statements lacking bias.

pacesetter: A person, group or thing that leads the way or serves as a model.

participant observation: A technique or process designed to collect information within a non-laboratory context that is at least partially determined by the observer's presence. Participant observation is therefore a methodology for design research. Its great advantage is that it allows for observation of groups with the self as a member of the group.

performance management: The use of information to help set agreed-upon performance goals and objectives, allocate resources, prioritize projects and activities, align functional projects/activities with strategic goals and business objectives.

performance measurement: The ongoing process of assessing progress toward achieving predetermined goals and objectives.

premium value: The highest value that can be achieved. This value is reached when a client recognizes great talent, an unusually valuable process, or the potential for synergy in a relationship.

process: A carefully considered, precisely controlled and constantly improved sequence of steps or operations leading to a predetermined result (Office Productivity). Example: Hypertrack Process.

process capital: The combined value of both value creating and non-value creating processes. Gives reason for reorganization of design teams.

process management: A philosophy and a way to lead and organize a firm. The firm's operations are looked upon as a set of processes whose purpose is to produce goods or services that satisfy customers.

process-driven organization: An organization structured so that processes will work effectively. This kind of organization has processes as its backbone and is not built up around activities or functions (Office Productivity).

profitability: Most firms tend to minimize profits for tax purposes. Therefore, profits before distributions and taxes are the most meaningful figures, and profits have to be adjusted for any unusual or nonrecurring events.

real time management: Management for real time business. Characterized by minimizing response time to new circumstances and customer expectations.

re-engineering: A radical redesign of business processes to achieve improved results. Leads to best practice or failure. Re-engineering requires leadership wisdom.

relationship value: Human capital assessed according to the value it might create in combination with structural capital (also social capital).

staff utilization ratio: The ratio of billable hours divided by the total hours for all staff, expressed as a percentage.

strategic objective: Strategic goals that are in line with the mission. Strategic objectives are high level goals that are divided into different focus areas in the balanced scorecard grid.

synergism: The simultaneous action of separate firms that, together, have greater total effect than the sum of their individual effects.

supply-chain management: Tracking the movement of and demand for components used to manufacture a product across a variety of potential and actual suppliers, otherwise known as the supply chain.

tacit knowledge: Tacit knowledge is highly personal and hard to formalize and communicate. Tacit knowledge consists of know-how and mental models, beliefs and perspectives (Ikujiro Nonaka).

team: A group of people working together with a shared vision.

team building: Visualizing benefits from working in a team context and thereby stimulating teamwork.

three-generation team (3 G-teams): Team consisting of cross-border members from different generations, professional backgrounds, functions and cultures.

time to market (TTM): The time it takes from when a firm has defined a client need to when it can begin meeting it with a new service or a new generation of an existing services.

valuation: The process of assessing firm value, theoretically defined as the present value of all future cash flows discounted at the appropriate cost of capital.

value: A measure of appreciation of some phenomenon. The value of goods and services can either be measured by the amount of money or other goods or services for which they can be exchanged. Value is what someone wants and is willing to pay to get it.

value added: Operating result after depreciation, plus wage costs, payroll overheads and business development costs.

value chain: A generic model to analyze activities and costs in a company as well as in entities further up and down the chain. The model originates from work by Michael E. Porter.

value creation: Refinement and transformation of human capital, customer capital and organizational capital through mutual collaboration, into financial as well as non-financial value. A direct result of how people generate and apply knowledge.

value driver: An aspect of the organization that has been identified as providing significant future value; it indicates the firm's competitive advantage.

value networks: A social fabric for the fair exchange of tangibles and intangibles (Verna Allee).

values: Conceptions, explicit or implicit, distinctive of an individual or characteristic of a group, of the desirable which influences the selection from available modes, means and ends of actions. They are principles that you hold to be of worth in your life; who you are right now.

ABOUT THE AUTHORS

James P. Cramer, Hon AIA, Hon IIDA, CAE, is the chairman and CEO of the Greenway Group, a management consulting and research firm. He is the Co-founder of the Design Futures Council. Cramer is the author of three best-selling books on design management including *Design plus Enterprise: Seeking a New Reality in Architecture*. With Scott Simpson he co-authored the book *The Next Architect*. He is the founding editor and publisher of the journal *DesignIntelligence*. Cramer is the former executive vice president and CEO of The American Institute of Architects, Washington D.C. His work has been featured in *BusinessWeek, Architectural Record, The Wall Street Journal*, NPR's *All Things Considered*, and elsewhere. He is a Richard Upjohn Fellow of the AIA and a Senior Fellow of the Design Futures Counsel. He studied at Northern State (S.D.), University of St Thomas, University of Minnesota, and the Wharton School of Business, University of Pennsylvania.

Scott Simpson, FAIA, LEED AP, is Senior Director of KlingStubbins, a Jacobs Company. He is a Richard Upjohn Fellow of the American Institute of Architects and a Senior Fellow and co-chairman of the Design Futures Council. Simpson is the chairman of the Board of Overseers of the Boston Children's Museum and a Trustee of New England College. He has published more than 170 articles on issues of innovation and practice management and has co-authored two books, *The Next Architect, A New Twist on the Future of Design*, and *How Firms Succeed, A Field Guide to Design Management*, with James Cramer. He is Editor-at-Large of *DesignIntelligence* and is a frequent speaker at conferences and symposia, including the annual World Design Forum. Recently he has lectured at the Harvard Business School, Yale, Rice, Illinois, Montana, and Wisconsin's schools of architecture. He has degrees from Yale and Harvard.

ABOUT THE AUTHORS

James P. Cramer, Hon. AIA, Hon. IIDA, CAE, is the chairman and chief executive officer of the Greenway Group, a management consulting and research firm based in Atlanta. He is the author of *Design plus Enterprise: Seeking a New Reality in Architecture and Design*, co-author with Scott Simpson of *The Next Architect*, and editor of the monthly journal *DesignIntelligence*. Cramer is the founder and chair of the Design Futures Council and the former executive vice president/CEO of the American Institute of Architects in Washington D.C.

Scott Simpson, FAIA, LEED AP, is Senior Director of KlingStubbins, a Jacobs Company. He is also a Richard Upjohn Fellow of the American Institute of Architects, a Senior Fellow of the Design Futures Council, Chair of the Board of Overseers of the Boston Children's Museum, and a Trustee of New England College. Mr. Simpson has published more than 170 articles on issues of innovation in the A/E/C industry and has co-authored two boos, *How Firms Succeed: A Field Guide to Design Management*, and *The Next Architect: A New Twist on the Future of Design*. he is a frequent speaker at national conferences and symposia and has been a guest presenter at the Harvard Business School and the Yale, Harvard, Rice, University of Illinois, University of Montana, and University of Wisconsin schools of architecture. He holds academic degrees from Yale and Harvard.

Notes

östberg

Library of Design Management

Every relationship of value requires constant care and commitment. At Östberg, we are relentless in our desire to create and bring forward only the best ideas in design, architecture, interiors, and design management. Using diverse mediums of communications, including books and the Internet, we are constantly searching for thoughtful ideas that are erudite, witty, and of lasting importance to the quality of life. Inspired by the architecture of Ragnar Östberg and the best of Scandinavian design and civility, the Östberg Library of Design Management seeks to restore the passion for creativity that makes better products, spaces, and communities. The essence of Östberg can be summed up in our quality charter to you: "Communicating concepts of leadership and design excellence."